GOING AGAINST THE WIND

GOING AGAINST THE WIND

A Pictorial History of
African-Americans in Atlanta

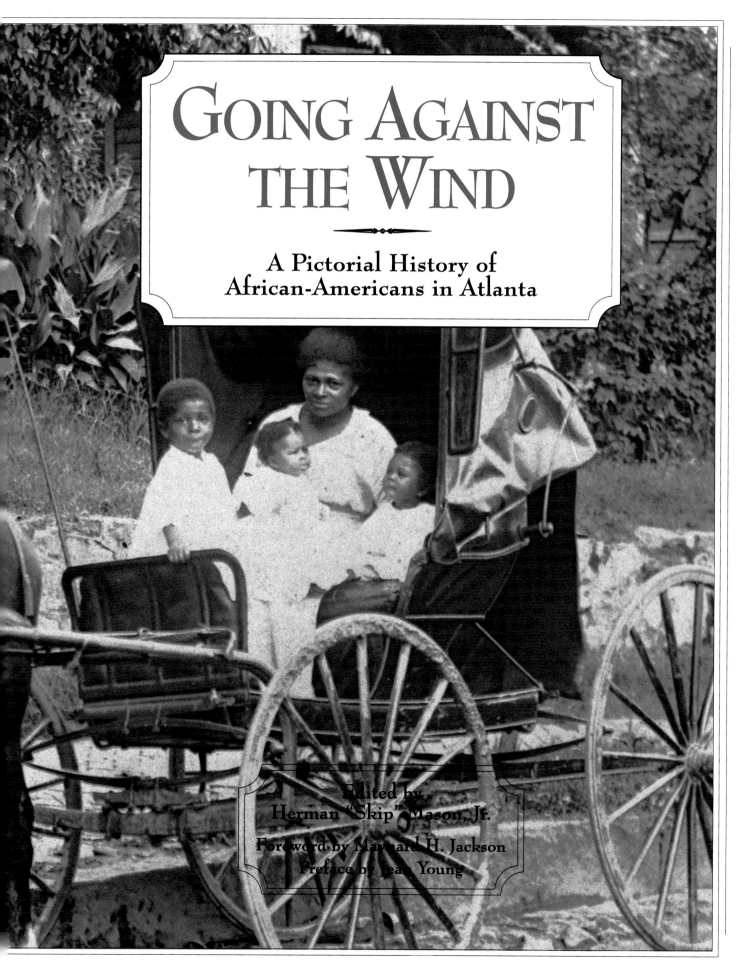

Edited by
Herman "Skip" Mason, Jr.
Foreword by Maynard H. Jackson
Preface by Jean Young

LONGSTREET PRESS
Atlanta, Georgia

Published by Longstreet Press, Inc.,
a subsidiary of Cox Newspapers, Inc.,
and the Atlanta Journal and Constitution.

This publication in a joint venture of
The Atlanta Journal and Constitution
and The APEX Museum (African-American
Panoramic Experience), Atlanta, Georgia
Compiled and edited by Herman "Skip" Mason, Jr.

Printed in the United States of America
1st printing 1992
ISBN 1-56352-061-3

This book was printed by Book Press, Inc., Brattleboro, VT.
The text was set in Garamond.

Book design by Laurie Shock.
Jacket design by Laurie Shock.

Longstreet Press, Inc.
2140 Newmarket Parkway
Suite 118
Marietta, GA 30067

CONTENTS

FOREWORD

Going Against the Wind captures in book form the stunning 1991 photographic exhibit at the APEX Museum entitled "Hidden Treasures: African-American Photographers, 1870–1970," which showcased the talents of these artists and revealed a vibrant, thriving African-American community in Atlanta. Exhibit Curator Herman "Skip" Mason, Jr., has taken the photographic history of our community as his subject in this volume, adding the works of white photographers and expanding the time frame to cover two hundred years (1793–1992).

From the antebellum years covered in Chapter 1 through the late-twentieth-century "Going for the Gold" years of Chapter 12, we discover black artisans, professionals, scholars, entrepreneurs, property owners, and civic leaders establishing and preserving our neighborhoods, organizing self-help associations to protect and uplift our families, creating the world's largest consortium of African-American colleges and universities to educate our children, and joining hands with white Atlantans to create what has come to be one of the premier cities of the world.

I am proud to discover in these pages the photographic record of my grandfather, John Wesley Dobbs, co-chairman of the Atlanta Negro Voters League, Grand Master of the Prince Hall Masons of Georgia for twenty-six years; my father, the Reverend Dr. Maynard H. Jackson, founder of the Georgia Voters League; other members of my family; our hero, Dr. Martin Luther King, Jr.; and so many more who have contributed much to the civil rights and the cultural, economic, academic, social, and political richness of this city for all Atlantans.

Many African-American Atlantans will discover their predecessors among these pictures that show us erecting the buildings and bridges, laying the streets and boulevards, and providing the skills, services, and aesthetic gifts that helped transform this city from Terminus to Marthasville to Atlanta. All Atlantans of every ethnic background can take pride in the record of achievement chronicled in these several hundred photographs.

As mayor of the city of Atlanta, I benefit from the many leaders of America's most extraordinary African-American community, Atlanta. Congratulations to Herman "Skip" Mason, the APEX Museum, the *Atlanta Journal and Constitution*, and Longstreet Press for this historic record. I commend *Going Against the Wind* to all who would know the full story of Atlanta's rise from ashes to greatness.

Maynard H. Jackson, Mayor
City of Atlanta

PREFACE

The image of black men and women working in cotton fields is the most prevalent perception of African-Americans in the Old South. This was not the work or lifestyle of many African-Americans. In Southern cities, blacks engaged in a wide variety of occupations and lived in many different ways. One could see on the streets of Atlanta laborers working on the railroad while ladies and gentlemen of color rode by in horse-drawn carriages.

This remarkable collection of photographs portrays the rich texture of life in Atlanta from its founding until the present. Skip Mason has gleaned hundreds of priceless pictures from the homes and attics of scores of Atlanta citizens to produce this outstanding book. Though the photographs tell the story, a detailed timeline of events satisfies readers who want further documentation.

The APEX (the African-American Panoramic Experience) is a different kind of museum in that it seeks to correct many of the misconceptions, pervasive omissions, and inaccurate statements commonly recorded in books about the history and culture of African-Americans. The production of this book certainly helps to present a more balanced view than the popular *Gone with the Wind*. The title *Going Against the Wind* was thus purposefully chosen to reflect African-Americans' constant struggle to survive in a society fraught with discrimination and adversity. In seeking to fulfill its mission to depict African-Americans accurately, the APEX commissioned Skip Mason as writer and editor and joined with the *Atlanta Journal and Constitution* and Longstreet Press to produce this book. Every family in Atlanta should be proud to display this moving collection of photographs and commentary in their homes.

The APEX board, staff, and volunteers are committed to presenting a true and accurate portrayal of African-Americans. With more knowledge, our young people will enhance their self-image, and our citizens will gain more appreciation and understanding of African-American culture and history. Perhaps this will foster greater cooperation and racial harmony among our citizens.

Representing the APEX Board of Directors, along with Dan Moore, founder and executive director, I enthusiastically present this unprecedented pictorial document to the citizens of Atlanta and all who desire more knowledge of the African-American experience.

Jean Young, Chair
The APEX Museum

ACKNOWLEDGMENTS

This pictorial history of the African-American community in Atlanta is an offspring of an exhibition I curated at the APEX Museum in 1991. Entitled "Hidden Treasures: African-American Photographers in Atlanta, 1870—1970," it presented to Atlantans over three hundred images of "Black " Atlanta as seen through the eyes of the photographers.

First, let me acknowledge my former supervisor, Janice White Sikes, for planting the seed of pictorial history in my mind following the exhibit. I also would like to thank Joyce Jelks and the Board of Directors of the African-American Family History Association for their initial support.

Special thanks go to Dan Moore, founder and president of the APEX Museum, Bethany Campbell (director, Phase I), Pat Bynton, and and APEX Board Chair Jean Young for their belief in my abilities to complete this task. At the Atlanta Historical Society, I am grateful to Ted Ryan and Bill Hull, and Peter Roberts at Georgia State University, whose spirit of cooperativeness and willingness to pull wonderful unpublished images from their great collections helped bring this book to life. I also appreciate the help of Gail Miller at the Georgia Department of Archives and History. Of course, a book of this nature could not be published without the assistance of Dovie Patrick and Minnie Clayton in the Special Collections Department of the Robert Woodruff Library in the Atlanta University Center. To Sharon Robinson, a big thanks for her assistance and insight.

At the *Atlanta Journal and Constitution,* I am grateful to librarians Diane Hunter and Kathryn Walker, who opened up the newspapers' wonderful photo collection for me. A special thanks also goes to the photo staff—Ricks Addicks, Pam Prouty, and Connie Woods—for their cooperation and expeditious response to my requests. To Alexis Scott Reeves and David Scott of Cox Newspapers, my deepest appreciation for making this project a reality. To Chuck Perry, Suzanne Comer Bell, and the staff at Longstreet Press, many thanks for their expertise in shaping this project into a book. Much gratitude to Casper L. Jordan, for reading the manuscript; to Anita Harvey, for sharing her writing skills; and to Mozell Powell and Jackie Sykes, who typed the manuscript, for their efficiency and patience. Thanks to Diane Leasure, Bill Mennoah, and the skillfull technicians at Prizma Photographic for their wonderful work.

My most humble thanks go to the known and unknown photographers, both black and white, whose works are featured in the publication. Their names are listed following the last the bibliography. A generous thanks, also, to the contributors of the photographs, for sharing many wonderful images from their personal collections, without whom this book could not have been possible.

A project of this magnitude would not have been possible without the love and support of family and friends, who are too numerous to name. A special thanks always to my mother, Deloris, and sister Dionne for their love, and to Rev. Jerome B. Price and the Westside Church family for their prayers.

I dedicate this book to the memories of the late Othello "Chico" Renfroe, Grace Towns Hamilton, Alex Haley, and my late grandmothers, Lola Mae Harris, Elizabeth Mason, and Mary Conley, who were wonderful storytellers of days gone by. I also dedicate it to my godson, David Alexander Smith. And, finally, to my niece Shakari Bodford, a fourth-generation Atlantan and a vibrant, energetic toddler who has already developed a love for picture books—this book is for you. When you learn how to read, you will then understand African-Americans in Atlanta have "gone against the wind" to make changes, promote racial harmony, and reclaim our inherited place as the original "movers and shakers" of this brave and beautiful city.

INTRODUCTION

Simply put, *Going Against the Wind* is a picture book, a compilation of unique and often rare photographs assembled to provide a visual documentation of the history of African-Americans in Atlanta. Though other pictorial histories on the subject have been written—including work by local historians Franklin Garrett, Norman Shavin, Dana White, and Dan Durett—this volume is the first comprehensive pictorial and chronological history of the African-American experience in the city. This is the first to document what Rev. Edward Randolph Carter called "The Black Side" in his pioneering book of the same title in 1894.

As I began to focus in on the project, my central question was, Why should there be a separate publication for African-Americans in Atlanta? Charles Dickens might have referred to Atlanta as "A Tale of Two Cities" or, as local historians Dan Durett and Dana White called it, "Another Atlanta." I believed that such a book should be compiled to provide a glimpse of how African-Americans have attempted to make progress and racial strides, fit into the mainstream of Atlanta society, and carve out their own niche.

Focusing on the seat of the civil rights movement and, by media reports, one of the ten most attractive cities for African-Americans in the country, this pictorial and chronological history will provide to natives, newcomers, transplants, and tourists a visible record of our being. Furthermore, it is an attempt to dispel myths about the "Negro presence in Atlanta." Contrary to what others have recorded, African-Americans did not go with the flow, or blow with the winds of Jim Crowism.

Thousands of tourists flock to Atlanta looking for mint juleps, remnants of Scarlet O'Hara and Rhett at Tara, and, of course, their beloved Mammy. The novel and movie *Gone With the Wind* have done more than any other media to present an image of Atlanta to the world. Even at the premier of the movie in 1939 at the Lowe's Grand Theater, a local African-American church choir performed spirituals in traditional slave dress, albeit dungarees, bandanas, and the like giving credence to the ways of the Old South.

Atlanta is the home of the largest consortium of African-American colleges and universities in the world and has witnessed the development, growth, and subsequent decline of what *Forbes* magazine described in 1956 as the "richest negro street" in America, Auburn Avenue. Still, there remains a mystique to and a lack of knowledge of and the roles that African-Americans have played in Atlanta since its creation as a hub for railroad transportation. Not only did African-Americans build the tracks that carried the railcars and its cargo throughout Georgia, but they were also the craftsmen and laborers who helped rebuild the city after Sherman's disastrous march.

Today, a large percentage of the African-American population in Atlanta has "transplanted" to the city "too busy to hate." Unfortunately, only a few publications accurately and properly document the fascinating history of African-Americans in Atlanta. Contrary to general knowledge, the boundaries of historic "Black Atlanta" extend beyond Auburn Avenue, and there are hundreds of men and women whose names, works, and contributions have gone virtually unnoticed.

The published history of African-Americans in Atlanta has been sporadically written. Not since Reverend Carter published *The Black Side* in 1894 has there been a comprehensive study of Black Atlanta. Though many articles in the *Atlanta History*, the journal of the Atlanta Historical Society, include information on African-Americans, no one has undertaken a comprehensive historical account. This publication will begin to make a dent in that much-needed documentation.

Distinguished scholars such as W. E. B. DuBois, who early in the century studied the African-American community while teaching at Atlanta University, have offered a scholarly glimpse of an undocumented "Negro" Atlanta. In 1911, the Negro Business League of Atlanta published *The Negro Business Directory and Commercial Guide of Atlanta,* an attempt to consolidate on paper the vast amount of businesses operated by African-Americans in the city. Certainly, this was indeed a predecessor to the current publication "The Black Pages." In 1937, the Atlanta Negro Chamber of Commerce published the booklet "Atlanta, You Ought to Know Your Own," in which noted African-American citizens wrote the history of various areas, including religion and sports.

Numerous dissertations, theses, and papers have also added to the wealth of information compiled on African-Americans in Atlanta and are available at academic and public libraries in Atlanta. Several Atlantans were working on histories of Black Atlanta but were met with an untimely death. They include Alice Dugged Cary, the first librarian for the Auburn Branch Library, who died in 1923; and John W. Calhoun, former city councilman, businessman, and legend.

Though we are proud to present the first comprehensive history of African-Americans in Atlanta, we in no way mean to pretend that this is the final book on the subject. We regret any omissions or errors that we might have made and welcome all corrections for future editions.

Perhaps after the photographs stimulate you visually and the captions and chronology arouse your interest in the people's lives, you will want to seek out some of the sources listed in the bibliography and read more about African-Americans' history in Atlanta. I believe that each photograph is the subject of its own individual book.

We present this volume about a "race" in a city whose march for dignity and respect has seen African-Americans always "going against the wind," yet always prevailing.

GOING AGAINST
THE WIND

Chapter 1

Indians Out, White Man In, Slaves Travel Along for the Ride, 1793–1865

I am disgusted with negroes and feel inclined to sell what I have.
I wish they were all back in Africa or Yankee land.
To think that this cruel war was waged for them.

S. P. Richards, Atlanta, Georgia, 1863

1793 All immigrant free persons of color are required to register within thirty days of their entry into Georgia.

1818 Free African-Americans are required to register annually within the county of their residence.

1838 More than 16,000 Cherokee Indians are forced to migrate west on what became known as the "Trail of Tears."

1840 Col. Lemuel P. Grant (for whom Grant Park was named) gives Ransom Montgomery and other African-Americans property on which to erect their own place of worship. (A site was selected on Jenkins Street, where the church stood until Federals destroyed it during the Civil War. Colonel Grant returned the site to them, but it was sold and property on Wheat Street [later Auburn Avenue] was purchased. Named Old Bethel, the erected house of worship later was named Bethel Church and finally Big Bethel African Methodist Episcopal Church.)

There are 6 "free" persons of color, 952 male slaves, and 1,052 female slaves in Terminus. (Terminus was part of DeKalb County.)

1847 After two attempts, citizens of Marthasville receive a charter to change the town's name to Atlanta. (The population of Atlanta was 500, most of whom were employed by the Western & Atlantic Railroad.)

1848 Slaves receive permission to attend the First Baptist Church in Atlanta. They are seated in the balcony.

1850 Total population in Atlanta: 2,569. Slaves: 493. "Free negroes": 18.

"Blind Tom" Bethune is the most extraordinary figure on the Atlanta concert stage. (Bethune reportedly was the son of slaves and the property of T. G. Bethune, a south Georgia plantation owner.)

1851 A city ordinance forbids free African-Americans to walk with a "cane club" or to wear a cloak unless blind or infirm. (It was feared that the cane might be used as a weapon, while the cloak could be used to conceal one. Free blacks convicted of misdemeanors of wearing a veil or smoking a pipe or cigar in public were given a maximum of thirty-nine lashes.)

African-Americans cannot be out on any street, lane, alley, or other places without a permit after 10:00 at night.

Henry Long, a runaway slave from Richmond, Virginia, is arrested for making insurrectionary speeches in Atlanta. (His capture was in accordance with the Fugitive Slave Law of 1850.)

1852 The Atlanta City Council rules that slaves are required to have written permission to possess liquor. (If found violating this order, a slave received thirty-nine lashes to the back.)

Free African-Americans in Atlanta begin to pay an annual poll tax of five dollars per person.

1853 A slave named Frank, owned by William H. Graham of Stone Mountain and hired out at Dr. Thompson's Atlanta Hotel, kills his master and is indicted by a DeKalb grand jury on July 11, 1853. (Frank was found guilty and hanged. His crime was the only known reported incident of slave retaliation in DeKalb County, then a part of Marthasville.)

It is against the law to "hire, bind, or deliver" any horse, buggy, or carriage to free African-Americans without a written order from their guardians.

African-Americans are forbidden to gamble or carry firearms, other weapons, or any poisons. (The penalty was a fine. Failure to pay fines resulted in "such free person" being sold for time, as labor would pay the amount.)

Free African-American hotel porters in Atlanta are not allowed to solicit incoming train passengers to stop "for entertainment" at their places of employment. (Penalty was fifty lashes to be inflicted by the city marshall for which the guardian had to pay one dollar.)

1854   The City Council agrees to allow a slave, Ransom Montgomery, to sell coffeecakes in the passenger depot to accommodate passengers.

Slaves Leitha and Eunice Allen are arrested for arson, tried, convicted, and severely whipped.

1855   Three petitions are made from white citizens to bring free African-Americans into Atlanta. (The petitions were indefinitely postponed.)

1856   July. Mary Combs becomes the first African-American to acquire property in Atlanta. She buys a lot "in fee simple" for $250.

The city council denies a black man's "unwise" petition to open an ice cream saloon.

The city council receives a request from a group of local African-Americans to receive musical instruction from a Mr. Smith. (The request was turned over to the council's police committee.)

1858   Two hundred citizens present to the city council a document chastening African-American mechanics whose masters reside in other places and pay nothing for the support of city government.

1859   May 20. The city council orders that free blacks post bonds of $200 to live in Atlanta; failure to do so makes them liable to indenture.

Dentist Roderick Badger, a former slave, is denied the opportunity to practice.

Local slave dealers protest outside competition and demand higher city license fees for slave traders.

A free woman, Mary Combs, purchases property on the corner of Wheat and Peachtree streets. (She later sold the property and used the money to purchase her husband's freedom.)

Ransom Montgomery saves the lives of more than one hundred passengers as their train crosses a burning bridge over the Chattahoochee River. (For his heroic act, the state of Georgia gave Montgomery his freedom, and he purchased land near downtown Atlanta.)

Other African-Americans—Bob Webster, Dougherty Hutchins, and Jacob Nelson—purchase land in Atlanta.

The slave population is 3,000, 25 percent of the total population of Atlanta.

1860   Clarke & Grubb, wholesale grocers on Whitehall Street, commission merchants and Negro brokers, retain all classes of "negroes," and are paying the highest market price for all goods that may be offered.

Free blacks number 25 among residents of the city of Atlanta.

Peter Eskridge, a former slave in Jackson County, comes to Atlanta and later opens a grocery store on Wheat Street.

1861   The Atlanta Freedmen's Bureau Office is given a building by the federal government that was formerly "captured Confederate property." (The building was placed on rollers and moved down Houston Street to the northwest corner of Calhoun Street and Piedmont Avenue. Named Storrs School, it provided elementary education to African-American children and was torn down in 1923.)

A tax of $100 is imposed on all Negro mechanics whose owners reside out of the city of Atlanta.

A slave yard is operated by Robert Clarke. His slaves are trained mechanics, coachmen, cooks, house servants, and field hands.

Crawford, Frazier & Co. offers "a choice lot" of strictly prime young women, boys, and fellows for sale.

1862   Rev. Frank Quarles organizes the First Colored Baptist Church with twenty-five members. (Services were held initially in a boxcar near Walton Street. The church later moved to Luckie Street and eventually settled on the corner of Haynes and Markham streets. With increasing membership, they purchased property on West Mitchell Street and renamed their congregation Friendship Baptist Church.)

Mary Combs, the first African-American to purchase property in Atlanta, sells her lot for $500, double the amount she paid for it.

1863   Male slaves are levied to contribute to manual labor for work on Atlanta Fortification. (They were hired at one dollar per working day, which was paid to their respective owners.)

Slave dealer Robert A. Crawford, located at 10 Peachtree Street, claims to have the most extensive "Negro" depot in the Confederacy.

Slave pricing occurs. (The end of the Civil War created a "bonanza" for slaveholders. One price was quoted at $2,000.)

1865   May 13. Union colonel B. B. Egleston orders that all blacks found without passes within the city limits will be arrested and jailed.

May. Owners or employers of Negroes are required to furnish them with proper passes. (Subject to arrest and confinement if found without passes within the city limits, many African-Americans began fleeing Atlanta and heading north with the "Yankees.")

July 14. The city council adopts an ordinance promising equal application of laws to whites and blacks.

A major Atlanta newspaper reports that African-Americans are living in the "most abject wretchedness everywhere, and living in idleness, vice and profligacy."

Atlanta citizens oppose Negro suffrage and express sympathy for the Negroes and support the policy of President Andrew Johnson.

The *Atlanta Intelligencer* cites that "ex-slaves" are now becoming a grave problem. (A rumor surfaced among "negroes" that come Christmas, the white folks' land would be divided and all "negroes" would have their share, commonly estimated at forty acres and a mule.)

The first black private school, the "Box-Car" school, is founded by the pioneer of black education in Atlanta, Rev. Frederick Ayer. (Opened by ex-slaves James Tate and Gradison B. Daniels at Walton Springs, it gave Atlanta two black schools.)

The Freedmen's Bureau is given a two-story building. (The building was dedicated in 1866 to the cause of elementary education for black children.)

A. J. Delbridge, a former slave from Notasulga, Alabama, moves to Atlanta and begins a prosperous shoemaking business.

Displaced and destitute families live in tents set up by the Freedmen's Bureau. They name the area Shermantown.

The Atlanta Medical College maintains a smallpox hospital for freedmen. City councilmen angered at the school's misuse of public funds cause the college to abandon the clinic. (Later, the Freedmen's Bureau established a hospital outside the city limits "to promote harmony among the citizens and this bureau." Ninety-six African-Americans were in the Freedmen's Bureau hospital.)

Relief societies such as Sisters of Honor and Brothers of Aid are established to supply food, clothing, and firewood to African-Americans in Atlanta.

On Whitehall Street was a facility that auctioned and sold African-Americans, 1860s.

Dr. Roderick D. Badger, Atlanta's first African-American dentist, was born in DeKalb County in 1830. He worked as an itinerant rural dentist, traveling from county to county. He lived in the Panthersville district of DeKalb County until 1856, when he came to Atlanta to practice. He worked on Sundays to pay for his instruments. A petition from several white Atlanta citizens was presented to the city council aggrieved that a "negro dentist" was allowed to work in Atlanta. Dr. Badger continued to work. During the Civil War, Dr. Badger served as an aide to a Confederate army colonel. He later served on the Board of Trustees for Clark University and owned an extensive amount of property in Atlanta. His office was located on Peachtree Street and his home was on east Harris Street. Dr. Badger died on December 27, 1890, and was buried in Oakland Cemetery.

Dr. Roderick D. Badger

African-Americans built shelters in an area they called Shermantown, named for General William Tecumseh Sherman, who destroyed Atlanta by fire during his treacherous march to the sea.

The scattering of African-Americans in Atlanta after the war saw the ruins of railroad roadhouses. Pictured in the foreground are the Atlantic Railroad and the West Point Railroad.

Solomon Luckie, a well-known African-American barber, while standing on the corner of Whitehall and Alabama streets in 1864, was injured when a shell struck a lamppost, ricocheted, and exploded. The fragment that hit him knocked him down. He was taken to the Atlanta Medical College, where his leg was amputated. He died a few hours later. The lamppost was restored to its original site at the northeast corner of Whitehall and Alabama streets in 1880.

Unidentified African-American Atlanta, c. 1865.

Chapter 2

"I'll Find a Way or Make One," 1866–1879

*The Negro had to consider themselves the shoe soles
and the whites the upper leather.*

Ransom Montgomery, a former slave who was given
property in Atlanta for a heroic deed in 1840

CHRONOLOGY

1866
A brush arbor is established at the corner of Martin and Crumley streets in Summerhill. It evolves into Woods Chapel in the spring, and Elder J. A. Woods is designated to organize an African Methodist Episcopal denomination in the community. (The church later relocated to Clarke and Fraser streets and was renamed Allen Temple A.M.E. Church.)

James Tate opens a grocery store on Walton Street with a total of $6.00 worth of stock. (Tate also operated and taught at a school in Old Bethel Church on Auburn Avenue.)

Madison and Sarah Reynolds and their seven children move from Covington, Georgia, to a small settlement between Atlanta and Decatur. (The community was eventually named Reynoldstown for this family. Their son Isaiah P. Reynolds, Sr., built a two-story brick store on the corner of Wylie and Kenyon streets in southeast Atlanta.)

1867
September. Frederick Ayer forms an African-American public school. (Initially named after him, the school was later called Summer Hill School.)

James Tate

Gen. John Pope issues order giving African-Americans the right to serve on juries.

Frederick Ayer and Edmund Ware petition for a charter to found Atlanta University. (The original land, purchased in 1869, was bought for $12,500. Its first students were all grammar and high school students.)

The Reconstruction Act allows African-Americans in Georgia to participate in Congress.

The Constitutional Convention assembles in Atlanta with Henry McNeal Turner, U. L. Houston, Madison Davis, Romulus Moore, Alfred Richardson, James Simm, Jacob Fuller, and thirty other African-Americans representing the concerns of African-Americans in Atlanta and Georgia.

A Board of Registration is appointed for each senatorial district in Atlanta consisting of two white men and one African-American man.

African-Americans in Atlanta are granted the right to vote. Federal troops begin registering them.

1868
African-Americans vote for the first time.

Local African-Americans request the hiring of a "black" policeman.

Mount Zion Baptist Church, the second African-American Baptist congregation in Atlanta, is founded.

1869
March 18. After expelling all blacks from its legislature in September 1868, Georgia now rejects the Fifteenth Amendment to the Constitution.

Rev. and Mrs. James W. Lee and the Freedmen's Aid Society of the Methodist Episcopal Church organize a primary school that later becomes Clark University on Fraser Street.

Levi Morrison becomes the first African-American newsboy for the *Atlanta Constitution.*

The name Summerhill is given to the recently settled community by Armstead Walker Bailey, Sr., who chose that name over Baileyville. (Bailey purchased property on Richardson Street, upon which a portion of the E. P. Johnson Elementary School would be constructed.)

Atlanta University opens its doors on the site of a former battleground known as "Diamond Hill."

1870
January 10. Gov. Rufus Bullock calls the legislature to convene with members elected in 1868 attending. (African-Americans elected were later expelled.)

Atlanta University launches its second term. There are so many students that some dormitory rooms have five occupants.

Rev. William Finch, a tailor, and George Graham, a carpenter, are the first two African-Americans elected to the City Council.

Rev. Andrew Jackson and seven people organize the Mount Pleasant Baptist Church. (The first church edifice was a wooden structure built on the corner of Fort and Wheat streets. Wheat Street would later be changed to Auburn Avenue.)

Thomas Goolsby, a contractor, becomes the first African-American to purchase a home on Auburn Avenue. The house was located between Piedmont and Butler streets.

Augustus Thompson, a Mississippi-born slave and prominent blacksmith in Atlanta, organizes a lodge and initiates twenty-five other young businesses in Atlanta.

Atlanta's Negro population totals 9,929, comprising 25.3 percent of the total population.

There are 3,129 Negro schoolchildren in Atlanta. City Council passes an ordinance providing for their education in the school system.

Jackson McHenry is nominated for city councilman but is defeated by sixty votes.

During Rev. William Finch's term on the council, streets in African-American neighborhoods are improved and repaired, a sidewalk is laid near Bethel African Methodist Episcopal Church, and a measure is defeated to prohibit positioning the Atlanta University campus on Mitchell Street.

1871   The Saint James Lodge No. 4 Free and Accepted Masons receives its warrant to begin operation.

An African-American man is arrested at the polling place for the Fifth Ward, presumably for fraudulent voting. Other African-Americans try to set him free and are confronted by the police.

City Council abolishes the code ordinance where a dollar is paid for each arrest. Leaders state that the fee tempts officers to arrest African-Americans on the slightest pretext.

1872   The Atlanta Board of Education takes over the Storrs and Summerhill schools.

Control of the state government passes to the Democrats, and African-American voting declines.

1873   The Haynes Street School, the first public grammar school for African-Americans on the west side, opens. (It was later relocated to Mitchell Street.)

The Zion Hill Baptist Church is founded by Rev. Robert Grant. (It was later relocated to the corner of McDaniel Street and Georgia Avenue.)

1874   The Georgia Legislature promises an annual appropriation of $8,000 to Atlanta University. (Atlanta University's total budget was $6,740.)

1877   Henry O. Flipper, son of slave Festus Flipper, becomes the first black graduate of the U.S. Military Academy at West Point.

Rev. and Mrs. James W. Lee open what is now known as Clark University. (The school was renamed Clark College in 1941.)

Ten-year-old Moses Amos arrives in Atlanta on foot and finds employment working for a white pharmacist in his pharmacy on Auburn Avenue.

1878   The first African-American teachers pass the school board examination and are hired.

1879   A saintly, distinguished, white-bearded member of Big Bethel called Brother Matthews is known by inhabitants of Old Fourth Ward as the bell ringer. (Parents rushed their kids off to Sunday school when this bell was rung every Sunday morning.)

The Augusta Institute moves to Atlanta and is renamed Atlanta Baptist Seminary. Classes are held at Friendship Baptist Church. (A year later the school moved into a new building on the corner of West Hunter and Elliot streets.)

A view of Atlanta's railroad tracks facing Marietta Street, 1870s.

Unidentified images of African-Americans in Atlanta following the war, c. 1866 (on the next four pages).

A view of the Union Depot and surrounding buildings from the State House, 1870s.

*Atlanta University, founded in 1865 by the American Missionary Association, offered a rigorous academic curriculum for its college depart-
ment and structured skills for its normal school.*

Chrisman Hall on the campus of Clark University was located in south Atlanta, c. 1879.

The Good Samaritan Building was located on Ivy Street.

The first Odd Fellows Hall was located on Piedmont Avenue.

Thomas E. Askew, a native of Georgia posed here with his sons, was Atlanta's first African-American photographer. He was trained by C. W. Motes, a successful portrait photographer, and operated his studio from his home on Summit Avenue. The Askew family were members of First Congregational Church. He died in 1914 and is buried in Oakland Cemetery. Three years after his death, the Great Fire of 1917 destroyed all of his photographic equipment and negatives.

Rev. William Finch, a former slave, was trained as a tailor and operated a successful business on Peachtree Street. A member of the Republican party, he was elected to the city council in 1870 as a representative of the Old Fourth Ward. He advocated public education for African-Americans.

Armstead Walker Bailey, a pioneer African-American settler. Bailey gave the name Summerhill to the community in which he and his family settled in 1869.

Antoine Graves, Sr., a pioneer realtor and former principal at Storrs School, strove to uplift the African-American race in Atlanta. When he received a request to close his school down and march along with his pupils in a parade honoring Confederate president Jefferson Davis, he resigned and moved to California. He returned shortly thereafter and opened offices in the Kimball Building on Wall Street, a street totally occupied by white Atlantans. Graves sold land throughout Atlanta, including a tract purchased by the Atlanta Board of Education to build the David T. Howard School.

African-American men served as drivers of surreys for many of Atlanta's wealthy and aristocratic whites, 1870s.

A family portrait of the Luckie family, 1870s.

Chapter 3

"Cast Down Your Buckets Where You Are," 1880–1899

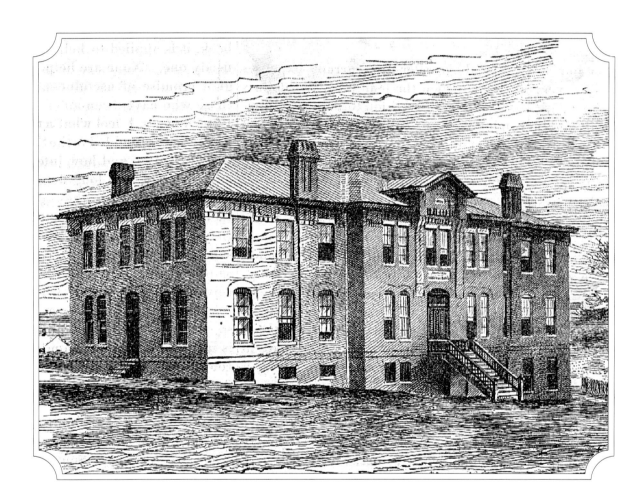

There is in this world no such force of a man determined to rise:
The human soul cannot be permanently chained.

W. E. B. DuBois

CHRONOLOGY

1880 Henry Rucker serves as a delegate from Georgia to the Republican National Convention in Chicago.

The city of Atlanta builds an eight-room school for African-American children on the corner of Houston and Butler streets in the Fourth Ward area.

1881 Atlanta Baptist Female Seminary is founded by two women from New England. These women petition for funds from John D. Rockefeller. (The school's name was later changed to Spelman Seminary in honor of Mrs. Rockefeller's mother. The school finally became Spelman College in 1924.)

Willis Murphey, a former slave from Jonesboro, opens a business on Decatur Street.

Morris Brown University is founded in the basement of Big Bethel A.M.E. Church. Mary McCree is the first principal. Bishop Wesley J. Gaines contracts with the Armstrong Soap Company for the school to receive a percentage of all proceeds from soap sold during a certain period. (From this percentage, the university's first building was erected in 1885.)

1882 The West Hunter Street Baptist Church is organized by Rev. J. A. McAllen with a membership of three.

From April to July, an epidemic of smallpox breaks out in the Beaver Slide community, with 120 cases reported.

Rev. S. E. Poe organizes the first Colored Methodist Episcopal Church in Atlanta on Butler Street. It is named Butler Street C.M.E. Church.

Mitchell Street School is erected near Maple and Mitchell streets in the First Ward.

1883 Gammon Theological Seminary opens.

1884 Wesley Chapel Redding and his family become the first African-American family to move to Auburn Avenue east of Boulevard. (Redding worked as a bank teller for African-American patrons at the Merchant Bank in Atlanta.)

Gammon Hall is dedicated on the campus of Clark University.

1885 The first class enters Morris Brown University on Houston Street and Boulevard.

Col. Floyd H. Crumbly, a former slave from Floyd County, starts his own business with a loan of $300 worth of goods from two white merchants.

1886 Rev. John Parker organizes the Ebenezer Baptist Church on Airline Street. (The church later purchased property on the corner of Auburn and Jackson streets.)

After the owner of a white Atlanta cemetery decides that African-Americans will have to use a back gate, Southview Cemetery is organized and incorporated at a meeting in the basement of Friendship Baptist Church by nine citizens: Nicodemus Holmes, C. H. Morgan, Albert Watts, Jacob McKinley, John D. Render, George W. Graham, William M. Allen, Annis J. Turner, and J. H. Towns.

Col. Floyd H. Crumbly

The Colored Men's Protection Association is organized by Rev. N. J. Jones to help those who are unable to help themselves.

Alice Dugged Cary is elected the second principal of Morris Brown College and is the second woman to hold the position.

1887 African-American schools are staffed entirely by African-American teachers and principals.

After passage of the Glenn Bill, making it illegal for African-American schools to admit white students, Atlanta University refuses to accept the provision requiring segregation. Its annual state fund of $8,000, appropriated to the school since 1874, is withdrawn.

Henry Rucker purchases a home on Piedmont Avenue.

1888   Victoria Maddox becomes the first graduate from Spelman Seminary High.

Atlanta Baptist Seminary (Morehouse College) purchases a fourteen-acre tract of land at West Fair and Chestnut streets.

The Committee of Seventy includes eighteen African-Americans. They make four requests for African-American appointments: two detectives and two drivers to the police force; four members to the Board of Education, two clerks in the county courthouse, and a candidate for city council.

1888–89   Henry O. Tanner teaches freehand drawing and painting. His private classes, held at Clark University and elsewhere, include white and African-American students.

1889   Carrie Steele, former maid at the Union Depot, sells her home and opens the Carrie Steele Orphans Home on Auburn Avenue. (She asked the city of Atlanta for financial assistance and was allowed to use the property rent-free, but the city did not offer her any additional support.)

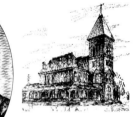

Carrie Steele and the Carrie Steele Orphans Home

Moses Amos, Thomas Heathe Slater, and Henry Butler buy out a drugstore on Auburn Avenue and rename it the Gate City Drugstore.

1890   The Leonard Street Orphan Home is opened for underprivileged African-American girls in an original Fort McPherson barrack purchased from Spelman.

African-Americans organize the Georgia Real Estate Loan and Trust Company.

Atlanta's population of 65,533 includes 28,098 African-Americans, or 42.9 percent.

The *Atlanta Constitution* interviews Atlanta's wealthiest African-Americans. They include Dr. Roderick D. Badger, a dentist; Willis Murphy, a grocer; A. J. Delbridge, a shoemaker; James Tate, owner of a dry goods store; Peter Eskridge, a merchant; David T. Howard, an undertaker; and Floyd Crumbly, a merchant.

Peter F. Hogans purchases a lot on Greensferry Avenue and erects a two-story building to be used as a grocery and storehouse.

Gray Street School is erected.

P. F. Hogans

African-American political leaders draw up an all "black" municipal ticket and keep it a secret. (It was leaked, however, to the local newspaper the day before the election, and white voters turned out in force to defeat all of the African-American candidates.)

African-Americans are treated for medical problems at the Ivy Street Hospital.

1891   The Atlanta Loan and Trust Company is organized by Wesley C. Redding and other African-Americans. It is located at the northeast corner of Bell and Auburn Avenue.

Former U.S. president Rutherford B. Hayes visits Atlanta University.

President Benjamin Harrison and explorer Henry Stanley visit Atlanta.

Henry Hagler organizes the *People's Advocate* newspaper, one of the first publications for blacks in Atlanta.

J. Robert Davis becomes one of the first, if not the first, African-American to pass the bar examination.

1892   Roach Street Grammar School is built to relieve overcrowded conditions in the Mitchell Street School.

Separation of races is legalized.

Civic leaders and clergymen lead a mass of African-Americans in a citywide streetcar boycott. (Similar boycotts occurred again in 1893 and 1900.)

1893   Atlanta City Council approves the renaming of Wheat Street to Auburn Avenue.

1894   J. S. Brandon begins plans to organize a Young Men's Christian Association. A group of young people meet in the basement of the Wheat Street Baptist Church to formalize the group. Brandon is elected president and his sister-in-law, Hattie Askridge, is elected organist. (The dominant action during the early years was song and prayer on Sunday afternoons.)

James Weldon Johnson, author of "Lift E'vry Voice and Sing," graduates from Atlanta University.

1895   The Atlanta Loan and Trust Company opens the European Hotel, the first hotel owned by African-Americans. (It was located on the corner of Auburn and Bell streets and was established to accommodate visitors to the Cotton States Exposition. Wesley Redding served as first manager of the hotel.)

A baseball team is organized at Morehouse College; players include Peter James Bryant, who would later become pastor of Wheat Street Baptist Church.

The first baseball team is organized at Morris Brown University; players include Charles Lincoln Harper and E. K. Nichols.

1896   Beulah Baptist Church is organized with three members by Rev. W. F. Paschal.

Dr. William E. B. DuBois of Atlanta University convenes the first of a series of conferences on the living conditions of urban blacks.

The barbershop owned by Alonzo Franklin Herndon and Doughtery Hutchins burns.

The first Atlanta baseball league is organized with Morehouse, Clark, and Morris Brown teams. Morehouse wins the first city title.

1897   The National Medical Association is organized by Drs. Henry R. Butler and Thomas Heathe Slater at the First Congregational Church.

The Union Mutual Insurance Association sets up headquarters in Atlanta, becoming the first chartered insurance association operated by African-Americans in the state of Georgia.

Henry Rucker is named by President William McKinley as collector of internal revenue, the only African-American to ever hold this position.

1898   The Fourth Atlanta University Conference on "The Negro in Business" is held.

Dr. W. J. Penn, brother of I. Garland Penn, moves to Atlanta and begins a medicine and surgery practice.

President Taft visits the First Congregational Church before reaching Big Bethel. (The Atlanta University Glee Club sang the "Star Spangled Banner," Bishop Wesley J. Gaines presided, and Professor William B. Matthews, principal of the Houston Street School, introduced President Taft.)

1899   Dr. W. E. B. DuBois and others protest the 1899 statute segregating sleeping cars on trains.

A view of Atlanta in the 1880s looking north down Peachtree Street.

The Main Building of Morris Brown University (changed to College in 1932) was located on the corner of Houston and Boulevard. The college was founded in 1881 in the basement of the Big Bethel A.M.E. Church as a result of a letter from Clark University inviting the A.M.E. trustees to occupy a room on its new campus. Trustee Steward Wylie asked, "If we can purchase a room at Clark University, then why can't we build a school of our own?"

Spelman students and faculty are lined up on the nine acres of drill ground used for the campus, 1880s. The army barracks in the background, which had housed federal troops during the Civil War, served as classroom and dormitory buildings. Spelman Seminary was founded in 1881.

Jackson McHenry, captain of the governor's Volunteer Army, ran unsuccessfully for the Atlanta City Council in 1870.

Residence of W. H. Landrum, owner of a hardware store on Decatur Street.

John W. Cox, a former shoemaker, opened a butcher's market and grocery store.

Rev. N. J. Jones organized the Colored Men's Protection Association in 1877.

Bishop Wesley John Gaines and his wife were very active in the religious, educational, and civic affairs of the African-American community in Atlanta during the turn of the century. They resided on Auburn Avenue.

Before Henry Ossawa Tanner sailed off to Paris in 1891 to further his art studies, he attempted to operate a photography studio in south Atlanta in 1889. After his venture proved unsuccessful, he taught art at Clark University, which was then located in the Brownsville community.

Unidentified yardman of Joel Inman, c. 1890.

Graves Hall, on the campus of Atlanta Baptist College (Morehouse College), was erected in 1889.

Many African-American women during the 1800s worked as nursemaids. The two ladies pictured here worked for Governor Coquitt at his home on the corner of Euclid and Moreland avenues, now Little Five Points, c. 1890.

African-American laborers built many of the railroad tracks in Atlanta during the early 1800s, helping the city become a major thoroughfare for railroad transportation. Here railroaders work on tracks at the intersection of Broad and Marietta streets, 1891.

*Mabel B. Johnson, teacher
at the Mitchell Street School.*

This young man stands in front of what is supposedly the first two-story house in Atlanta at 22 Trinity Avenue, c. 1891.

William B. Matthews

Fourth Ward Grammar School

Summerhill Grammar School

Fifth Ward Grammar School

Dohme and Duffy Gate City Tea and Coffee Company, located at 88 Whitehall Street between Hunter and Mitchell streets, was one of many businesses to employ African-American men as laborers and drivers, c. 1892.

African-Americans during the late 1800s flocked to the open-air markets located on Decatur Street near Union Station, which was built in 1871.

In 1894, Rev. E. R. Carter published The Black Side of Atlanta, *which chronicled the achievements of African-Americans in Atlanta.*

The home of Rev. and Mrs. E. R. Carter on Tatnall Street.

A scene from the International States Cotton Exposition, 1895. Note the African-American women in the background observing the bicyclist.

African-Americans throughout the country were attracted to the 1895 Cotton States Exposition held in Piedmont Park, which housed a Negro Building featuring exhibits and displays from all over the world.

It was during this exposition that Booker T. Washington, considered the "spokesman" for the race, electrified visitors with his "Atlanta Compromise."

Rev. Edward Randolph Carter (far right) and a group of people outside an unidentified Baptist church, c. 1890s. The church is not, however, Friendship Baptist Church, where he served as pastor for forty-five years.

*The president
in the Negro
Building at the
Cotton States and
International
Exposition,
Atlanta, Georgia.
Drawn by
W. A. Rogers.*

Many of the pioneering African-American families in Atlanta were of mixed ancestry, including Mr. and Mrs. Smith (seated). They were surrounded by Mrs. Thomas Askew (far right), her three daughters, and a friend (center), c. 1900s.

This little girl, Minnie B. Dyer, grew up to become a schoolteacher and in the 1920s and 1930s taught at the Old Ashby Street School (later renamed the E. R. Carter School). Her sister, Florine Dyer Furlow, was organist of Big Bethel A.M.E. Church for many years.

The sons of photographer Thomas E. Askew were very talented musicians, as seen in this photograph taken in the 1890s. Askew also had three daughters. Seated (l–r) are Clarence Askew, Arthur Askew, and Walter Askew. Standing are Norman Askew, Jake Sansome (a neighbor), and Robert Askew.

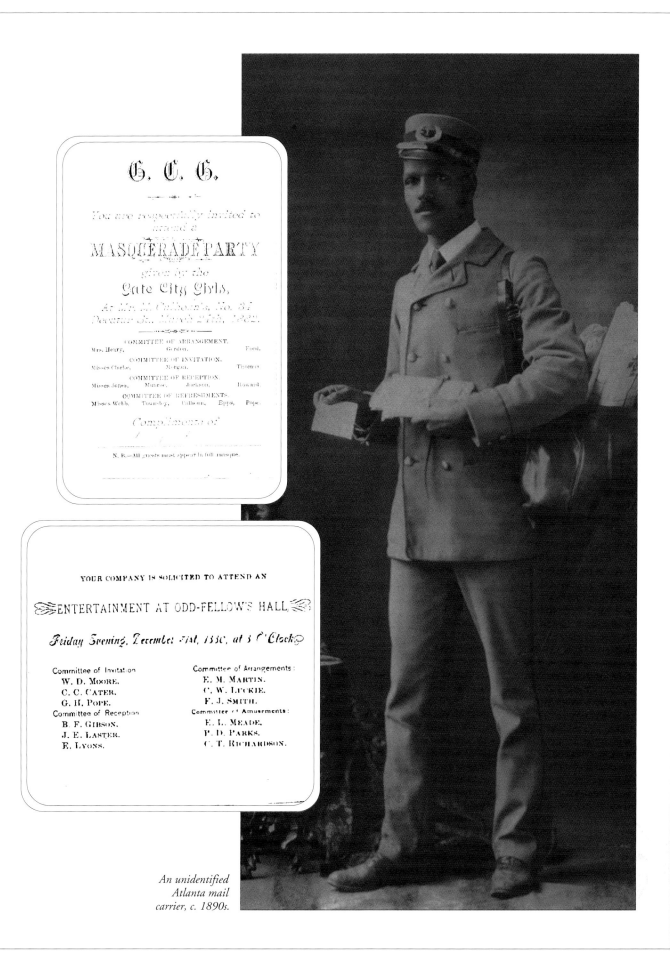

*An unidentified
Atlanta mail
carrier, c. 1890s.*

Being driven in his surrey is David Tobias Howard, the most successful undertaker of his time, along with his mother (left) and wife (right).

Streetcars headed to the International Exposition down an unidentified street, 1895.

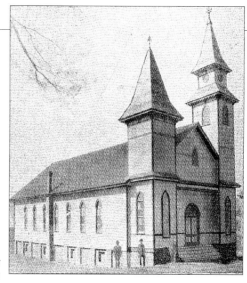

*Mount Olive
Baptist Church*

*Below: African-American
laborers laying pipe at an
unidentified site in Atlanta.*

First Congregational Church, located at the corner of Courtland and Houston streets.

Old West Hunter Baptist Church, founded in 1882 at the corner of Hunter and Chestnut streets.

Zion Hill Baptist Church, founded in 1873 and located on the corner of McDaniel Street and Georgia Avenue.

Second Mount Olive Baptist Church, located on Maple Street between Magnolia and Foundry streets.

Butler Street C.M.E. Church

A family portrait of the Henderson family, 1880s.

Chapter 4

Lifting the Race through Self-Help, 1900–1919

*N*o people ever got upon its feet and obtained the
respect and confidence of the world which did not lay its
foundations in successful business enterprises.

Booker T. Washington

1900   African-Americans in Atlanta boycott the Atlanta streetcars for eleven months protesting the city council's ruling requiring separate cars. Prominent African-Americans such as George A. Towns, professor at Atlanta University, and Peyton Allen, a prominent lawyer, buy bicycles rather than ride the segregated cars.

Emily Cox, an African-American woman, and her sons open the Cox Funeral Home on Auburn Avenue.

There are ten black companies, three black churches, and an orphanage on Auburn Avenue.

There are 35,727 African-Americans in Atlanta, comprising nearly 40 percent of all city residents.

The Twelve Club, a literary society, is formed.

Booker T. Washington organizes the National Negro Business League.

1901   Mrs. L. H. Holsey, wife of Bishop Lucius Holsey of the C.M.E. church, organizes the Holsey Temple C.M.E. Church.

An *Atlanta Journal* article criticizes the dinner invitation extended by President Theodore Roosevelt to Booker T. Washington. Roosevelt responds that the "Negro" is here to stay.

Benjamin G. Brawley, author of the *History of Morehouse College*, organizes the first football team at Morehouse College.

MacVicar Hospital is constructed on the Spelman Seminary campus.

Atlanta University professor George A. Towns accompanies Professor William E. B. DuBois to Tuskegee University for a conference on rural problems. Towns speaks out against those individuals who advocate only vocational training. Booker T. Washington disagrees with his remarks and has them stricken from the conference record.

1902   An Atlanta policeman is attacked by African-Americans in the Pittsburg area. The attack, known as the "Pittsburg Riot," involves three policemen; two African-Americans and one white man are killed.

Alonzo F. Herndon opens a barbershop at 66 Peachtree Street.

1903   *The Atlanta Independent*, a weekly newspaper published by the Grand United Order of Odd Fellows, appears.

The Negro Young People's Congress meets in Atlanta.

1904   Henry Rucker builds a five-story office building on the corner of Auburn and Piedmont avenues. It becomes the first office building for African-Americans in Atlanta.

Rev. Peter James Bryant organizes the Atlanta Benevolent and Protective Association, a small insurance society for members of Wheat Street Baptist Church and the community to provide relief in sickness and a decent burial at death. (The assessment fee ranged from 5 to 25 cents. Sick benefits ranged from $1 to $5 for a limited number of weeks, and death benefits ranged from $10 to $50. The office was originally located on Edgewood Avenue and later moved to the Rucker Building.)

Henry Lincoln Johnson begins his law practice.

1905   September 22–25. The Atlanta race riot occurs. Over five thousand whites are infuriated by alleged attacks on white women, as reported in a city newspaper. African-American streetcar passengers are killed near Five Points.

The Atlanta Mutual Insurance Association is formed by Alonzo Franklin Herndon, a successful African-American barber.

Alex Harvey opens the Silver Moon Barber Shop on Auburn Avenue.

The Gate City Kindergarten is organized by Gertrude Ware Bunce, Mrs. David T. Howard, Mrs. J. W. E. Bowen, Mrs. John Hope, and Mrs. Alonzo F. Herndon. The school is located on Cain Street and is funded by the First Congregational Church under the pastorship of Rev. Henry H. Proctor.

Four African-Americans from Atlanta attend the first conference of the Niagara Movement, a forerunner of the NAACP. They are George A. Towns, W. E. B. DuBois, John Hope, Alonzo Herndon, and Herndon's son, Norris.

A stronger state law threatens the existence of the Wheat Street Baptist Church's Atlanta Benevolent and Protective Association, and leaders of the organization approach Alonzo Herndon about purchasing the association for $140. He accepts the offer, reorganizes with two additional associations, and forms the Atlanta Mutual Insurance Association. The office moves to 202 Auburn Avenue.

President Theodore Roosevelt arrives in Atlanta, but his white sponsors do not permit him to visit any African-American colleges and universities. In his speeches, he does not discuss the "southern race problem," and, of the 50,000 African-Americans in Atlanta, not a single one is permitted by his committee to welcome him to the city.

1906

John Hope becomes the first African-American president of Atlanta Baptist College (now Morehouse College).

The National Negro Business League meets in Atlanta.

City council declares that partitions should divide white and black eating areas in barrooms.

1907

Col. Austin T. Walden is named assistant to the air raid director and is in charge of the African-American section in District Two of the Atlanta Municipal Defense Council.

Atlanta University sponsors the conference "Economic Cooperation among Negro Americans."

The Gayoso Electric Theater, located at 14 Central Avenue, is open for African-Americans.

J. E. and Henry Ivey establish the Ivey Brothers Funeral Home at the junction of Walker and Peters streets.

Asbury S. Williams has the grand opening of his photography gallery at 212 Auburn Avenue.

The Equal Rights League is organized for the purpose of registering "negroes" to vote against the disfranchisement amendment.

1908

The Neighborhood Union is created for African-Americans to promote health and recreation and to combat crime and juvenile delinquency. The agency is headed by Lugenia Burns Hope.

Violinist Antoine Graves travels throughout Georgia performing for whites-only audiences and giving in to racial prejudices in the literary and musical world.

1909

Dr. Carl M. Tanner, brother of renowned artist and former Atlanta resident Henry Ossawa Tanner, accepts the pastorate of Big Bethel A.M.E. Church.

The Grand United Order of the Odd Fellows purchases property at the corner of Fairlie and Popular streets for $21,400.

W. J. Trent is elected president of the YMCA and begins a campaign drive to raise money to erect a headquarters.

Reynoldstown, which developed between Atlanta and Decatur after the Civil War and was where freed slaves settled to build new lives for their families, officially becomes annexed to the city.

Mrs. Lugenia Burns Hope and other women organize a literary club called the Inquirers Club.

The Atlanta State Savings Bank is organized by African-Americans and located on Auburn Avenue.

Booker T. Washington breaks ground for the new building for the First Congregational Church at the request of its pastor, Rev. H. H. Proctor.

1910

July. The Great Colored Musician Festival—featuring Harry T. Burleigh, the Fisk Jubilee Singers, and others—is held at the Auditorium. Joseph Douglass, grandson of Frederick Douglass, performs a solo.

September. The Whitman Sisters, three African-American girls from Atlanta who reached national acclaim as entertainers and performers, return to Atlanta with an eight-person company to perform at the Jackson Street showgrounds.

October. Poet Thomas Jefferson Flanagan is introduced to the African-American community in Atlanta as a "literary genius" whose poetry and prose is compared to Paul Lawrence Dunbar. (His works appeared regularly in the *Atlanta Independent*.)

November. Morris Brown University organizes its first football team under Coach J. S. Jackson. Their first opponent is the Atlanta University Tigers. The *Atlanta Independent* makes a plea for a grandstand so that "colored" people will patronize the games.

Isom Speer, an African-American, owns an ice cream manufacturing store on Houston Street.

Dr. D. T. Dunbar, a graduate of South Bend College in Indiana, is the only African-American optician in Atlanta. His office is at 181 Auburn Avenue.

Dr. Homer F. Nash begins practicing medicine on Auburn Avenue.

Restaurants are "forced" to serve one race only and to designate which race with a prominently displayed sign.

African-Americans comprise 33.5 percent of the Atlanta population.

Dr. Hamilton M. Holmes, Sr., a recent graduate of Leonard School of Medicine (Shaw University), begins his medical practice in Atlanta and East Point, Georgia.

Daniel T. Robinson opens the first African-American printing shop in Atlanta on Auburn Avenue.

1911

June. Well-known contractor Alexander Hamilton dies.

President William Howard Taft speaks from the pulpit of Big Bethel A.M.E. Church.

The North Carolina Mutual Insurance Company opens a branch on Auburn Avenue.

The Negro Business Directory and Commercial Guide of Atlanta is published by the Negro Business Directory and Advertising Agency. William B. Matthews is proprietor.

The Honorable Alfred C. Sam of Gold Coast West Africa speaks to businessmen and leading African-American citizens at Big Bethel A.M.E. Church.

A published report shows that almost 75 percent of African-American children in Atlanta suffer one or more physical deficiencies, such as malnutrition, anemia, and glandular disease.

Selena Sloan Butler establishes the first African-American Parent-Teacher Association in Atlanta.

James Holloway opens Holloway Jewelers on Auburn Avenue.

1912

The Odd Fellows Building is dedicated.

1913

January. "The Old Shack," a piece of property at the corner of Fairlie and Popular purchased by the Grand United Order of Odd Fellows in 1909, is sold for $50,000, for a net profit of $30,000.

September 8. The Chautauqua Circle is organized by Mrs. Henrietta Curtis Porter, wife of pioneer dentist James Reynolds Porter.

September. The Hawk Hotel for African-Americans is operated by J. H. Hawk. (Located near the Old Union Shed Depot at 10 1/2 Central Avenue, it featured "hot and cold baths.")

December. Charles S. Cox, owner of Cox Funeral Home, purchases the Princess Theater, a local establishment for African-Americans. He promises to show "moving pictures" that have never been shown in "colored" theaters before.

The Atlanta Neighborhood Union, with Mrs. John Hope, president, affiliates with the National Urban League.

The Atlanta Baptist College is renamed Morehouse College for Dr. Henry Lyman Morehouse of the American Baptist Home Mission Board.

The Atlanta State Savings Bank becomes the first chartered African-American banking institution in Georgia. Some of its depositors include Standard Life, Atlanta Mutual, North Carolina, and Pilgrim Health and Life insurance companies. The officers and board of directors include the "movers and shakers" of Atlanta: David T. Howard, A. F. Herndon, Dr. Henry R. Butler, and Bishop Joseph S. Flipper. The president is J. O. Ross.

Atlanta copies Baltimore's premier residential segregation law of 1911, which legally establishes African-American and white neighborhoods, with the added proviso that a person of one color occupying a home in a mixed block could legally object to a person of another color moving next door.

Heman Perry, an agent with Massachusetts Mutual Insurance Company who came to Atlanta in 1908, starts the Standard Life Insurance Company, the first legal reserve insurance company in the world operated by an African-American.

Moses Amos becomes the first African-American pharmacist to receive a license in the state of Georgia.

Representatives from Southern colleges and universities meet at Morehouse College to form the Southeast Intercollegiate Athletic Conference, which would regulate intercollegiate athletics. Clark, Morehouse and Morris Brown are charter members. (The organization changed its name to the Southern Intercollegiate Athletic Conference in 1929.)

1914

March. Ware and Harper Realtors advertise lots for sale in University Park, a "strictly high-class 'colored' residential park" west of the Atlanta University schools. The lots are located on Ashby, Parsons, and Beckwith streets and Palmetto and Carolina avenues. The ad states that this property is to "colored" people what Peachtree Street, Ansley Park, and Druid Hills are to whites.

June 10. The Gate City Drug Store is opened in the new Odd Fellows Building by Dr. Moses Amos. Visitors receive ice cream and souvenirs.

August. The Eagle Steam Laundry, the first and only fully-equipped steam laundry owned and operated by African-Americans, opens at 221 Auburn Avenue.

Peters Street—lined with beer saloons, cheap eating joints, and bootleggers—is described as "one of the worst streets in the city." Adjacent areas include Beaver Slide, Fair Street, Roach Street, Whites Alley, Vine City, and Lightning. Many of these areas lack street lights, sewers, pavement, and water.

The *Atlanta Independent* features the founder of the ULACA Beverage Company, W. M. Fuller, a well-known African-American in Atlanta. His products are furnished to white grocers and soda water fountains throughout Atlanta.

Lots are advertised for Proctor Park on Ashby Street, a new subdivision. (The lots sold for $550. They were shown on Sunday afternoons, but no deals were closed on the Sabbath.)

The Gate City Barber Shop opens on Auburn Avenue.

1915
August. The Fulton Social Club is organized under the leadership of Col. Henry Lincoln Johnson and others to promote the social welfare of its members by fostering mutual acquaintances, providing social entertainments, and teaching the arts and graces of dancing, marches, and drills. (The club leased the Odd Fellows Roof Garden on Monday, Wednesday, and Friday nights of each week to furnish maids, chauffeurs, and all working people with a decent and moral atmosphere in which to obtain exercise and rest after a day's work. The club membership would grow to one thousand members in two years.)

September. Holmes Institute, located on Houston Street, opens to students who cannot attend public schools due to the inability of their parents to purchase books. Sewing, cooking, dressmaking, tailoring, millinery, and printing are taught, with special attention given to communications. Boarding can accommodate one hundred. The night school will open later. B. R. Holmes is president.

The 91 Royal Theater, a "refined picture and vaudeville house," opens on Decatur Street. Admission: 5 and 10 cents.

Charles Lincoln Harper, a graduate of Morris Brown University, becomes principal of Yonge Street Night School, the first evening school in Atlanta for African-Americans operated by the Atlanta Board of Education.

Charles M. Clayton begins as principal of the Sylvia Bryant Preparatory School on Auburn Avenue. One of his future students is Martin Luther King, Sr.

1916
June 26. Mrs. A. M. Pope Turnabo Malone, founder of Poro College of Scientific and Hair Treatment, shows moving pictures of her college at Wheat Street and Reed Street Baptist churches. Admission is 10 cents. Over 4,500 women are earning money selling her products throughout the country.

James A. Hopkins opens the Hopkins Book Concern.

Atlanta Life Insurance Company is incorporated.

The Atlanta Branch of the National Association of Colored Women's Club is founded by Lugenia Burns Hope.

1917
In the "great fire" of May 21, 1917, more than 1,938 houses in Atlanta are burned, and 10,000 people, mostly African-Americans, are left homeless. Property loss amounts to $5.5 million, of which $3.5 million is covered in insurance.

Grady Hospital hires Ludie Andrews, former superintendent of the Lula Grove Hospital Training School for Colored Nurses, to organize classes of "colored" nurses to relieve the strain on the white nurses at Grady. Her school is accredited.

Another steam laundry owned and operated by African-Americans, the Gate City Laundry, is built.

Fair Haven Infirmary opens on Irwin Street to train nurses and meet the needs of the African-American community. Two hundred and ten patients have been treated, and one hundred successful operations have been performed by leading African-American surgeons in the city. The infirmary is operated by Morris Brown University.

Ezella Mathis Carter, a graduate of the Mitchell Street School and Spelman Seminary, after taking a business course from LaSalle University in Chicago, takes three dollars and starts a company to manufacture cosmetic preparations. The company, Carter Manufacturing Company, employs over one thousand agents around the country selling the Carter System of Hair Culture to women in twenty-two states. Carter is also the editor of the *Women's Messenger*, a publication for African-American women.

1918
March. The Gate City Laundry reopens at 223 Auburn Avenue under the management of Cornelius King. King is also the proprietor and manager of a resort, King's Wigwam, in

Kennesaw, Georgia, for African-Americans.

May 1. W. C. Handy's Orchestra performs at the Auditorium and Armory on Courtland Street under the auspices of the War Council of Colored Women.

June 19. A prize fight between Jack Johnson and Sam Langford takes place at the Auditorium and Armory on Courtland Street. One half of the auditorium is reserved for "colored" people. Tickets range from $1 to $3, including war tax.

June. A notice appears in the *Atlanta Independent* of the intent to organize the Citizens Trust Company. The proposed corporators include Atlantans Heman Perry, James A. Robinson, H. C. Dugas, and George E. Haynes and Emmett J. Scott of Tuskegee Institute.

October. The Odd Fellows Roof Garden closes due to outbreak of the Spanish Flu in the African-American community.

One hundred and sixty-eight lots are advertised for sale in the Battle Hill District, two miles from the city on West Simpson Street. Buyers can pay $5 to $25 down and $41 per week.

James Weldon Johnson of the New York National Office of the NAACP assists Harry H. Pace, Truman K. Gibson, and other concerned citizens with the formation of the Atlanta Branch. Rev. A. D. Williams, pastor of Ebenezer, is elected president; Professor George A. Towns, vice president; and Dr. Leonidas Crogman, secretary. Meetings are held every Tuesday night.

The YMCA property on Auburn Avenue is sold for $7,200, and property is purchased on Butler Street for $10,609. (Built by Alexander D. Hamilton, the new structure cost $115,000 and contained over 10,000 square feet. It housed 48 dormitory rooms, 7 class rooms, a small auditorium, a gymnasium, a swimming pool, shower baths, a cafe, and restrooms.)

1919   May. Alpha Phi Alpha Fraternity, Inc., organizes the first African-American Greek letter fraternity in Atlanta. (The chapter was later dissolved and rechartered in May 1920. In December 1919, the Eta Omega Chapter of Omega Psi Phi was formed.)

June. Former grocers G. D. Parks and W. R. Parks open the Parks Loan and Investment Company on Whitehall Street.

July. One hundred lots on West Hunter Street are advertised in the *Atlanta Independent*. The lots are near the trolley car line and have paved streets, city water, and sewer.

September 4. A committee to form a Young Women's Christian Association meets at the Blue Triangle Center at 128 Piedmont Avenue. At the suggestion of Mrs. Selena Sloan Butler, the name of the group will be called the Phillis Wheatley YWCA, commemorating the first African-American poet.

The Southern Field Division of the National Urban League sets up its headquarters in Atlanta, with Jesse O. Thomas as the first director and Lemuel L. Foster the executive secretary. (Urban League activities in the region created a dire need for professionally trained social workers, and the Atlanta School of Social Work was established the following year.)

Cornelius King and Son, Realtors, is founded.

The first Negro league baseball team is organized in Atlanta as the Atlanta Black Crackers.

The Atlanta Branch of the NAACP assists in saving the life of Charles Harris, from Marietta, who allegedly killed his white landlord.

Skilled African-American laborers putting in second waterline at the Hemphill Pumping Station and constructing the waterline on Marietta Street, c. 1900.

The view of Atlanta in 1900 as seen from the state capitol dome.

The intersection of Peachtree and Marietta streets in the early 1900s.

This butcher's market is believed to have been located in the Summerhill area. Note the fish hanging over the door and the cutting saw in one of the worker's hands.

Though slightly blurred in the background, African-American workers are seated next to the John Smith Carriage Factory, 120–24 Auburn Avenue, where they were employed, c. 1903.

The Atlanta Terminal Station (c. 1910), at the corner of Mitchell Street and Madison Avenue (now Spring Street), attracted many Atlanta youths who sought to earn a few pennies by carrying bags and luggage. The station opened in May 1905 and had separate facilities for "Colored" riders. It was demolished in 1972 to make way for the Richard B. Russell Federal Building.

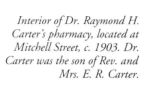

Interior of Dr. Raymond H. Carter's pharmacy, located at Mitchell Street, c. 1903. Dr. Carter was the son of Rev. and Mrs. E. R. Carter.

An unidentified African-American man is draped in Ku Klux Klan regalia on top of the Kelly Brothers Company automobile, c. 1905.

On the front porch of the Graves home are (l–r) Marie Woolfork (who would attend Howard University and become a charter member of the Alpha Kappa Alpha sorority), Nellie Graves, Catherine Graves, Mrs. Graves, and Marie Graves, c. 1905.

Montgomery, the little boy next to the horse, poses with the wagon of the Red Rock Distribution Company on Auburn Avenue, c. 1904. Founded in 1885, Red Rock employed numerous African-Americans, including Montgomery, who continued to work for the company as an adult.

The home of Antoine and Nellie Graves, 116 Howell Street, off of Auburn Avenue.

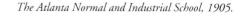

The Atlanta Normal and Industrial School, 1905.

These and other "Race Men" concentrated on improving the economic, educational, and political status of African-Americans at the turn of the century.

Robert E. Pharrow, who construct-ed the Odd Fellows Building

Benjamin Davis, founder and editor, Atlanta Independent

Edwin Driskell, owner, Union Mutual Publishing Company

Henry Hugh Proctor, pastor, First Congregational Church

Peter James Bryant, pastor, Wheat Street Baptist Church

W. E. B. DuBois, Ph.D., professor at Atlanta University

George Alexander Towns, professor, Atlanta University

John Wesley E. Bowen, president, Gammon Theological Seminary

Alonzo F. Herndon, owner, Herndon Baths and Barbers, and president, Atlanta Mutual Association

Joseph S. Flipper, bishop, A.M.E. church, and former pastor, Allen Temple and Saint Phillips A.M.E. Church

The African-American community rolled out the red carpet to host President William Taft. Rev. Henry Proctor, pastor of First Congregational Church, led the "negro delegation" during his visit. Note the interracial mixture of men on the steps of the church, c. 1909.

A view of the most magnificent edifice in the African-American community in Atlanta, the home of former slave Alonzo Franklin Herndon; his wife, Jessie; and son, Norris. The house was initially planned and built for Herndon's first wife, Adrienne Herndon, an elocution teacher at Atlanta University who died soon after the house was completed in 1910. Herndon married Jessie Gillespie, a beautician from Chicago, in 1912.

African-American workers constructing the Forsyth Building at the corner of Forsyth and Luckie streets, c. 1910.

1911

President William McKinley appoints Henry A. Rucker a collector of internal revenue. He serves in this position until 1909.

A young African-American walks past Pryor Street North from Hunter Street, c. 1910.

Brothers Frank (standing) and George Powell in the Auburn Photo Studio. The brothers resided in the Summerhill community.

Unidentified social gathering, 1910.

*The fiftieth anniversary celebration of David and Ella
Howard, c. 1913.*

The Atlanta Independent *served as the major communications source for African-Americans in Atlanta and Georgia. Established by the Grand
United Order of the Odd Fellows, the newspaper was edited by the outspoken and courageous Benjamin Davis.*

Moses Amos, standing at the corner of his business, the Gate City Drug Store. Amos was the first licensed African-American pharmacist in the state of Georgia.

Gate City Drug Store
Cor. Auburn Ave. and Butler St.
MOSES AMOS, Manager.
Phones: 1844

ATLANTA, GA. 2 — 14 — 1913

This is to certify that we, C. C. Cater, Thos. H. Slater, and F. J. Wimberly agree to sell our interest in the Gate City Drug Store (in the county of Fulton, and state of Ga.) to Moses Amos of the county of Fulton for $1000.00 One thousand dollars. He, Moses Amos) assuming all indebtedness of the above named Gate City Drug Store, and relieving us from any and all liabilities whatever pertaining to the said Gate City Drug Store in the event that (He, Moses Amos) agrees that at the launching of the new corporation that a published account of the dissolution of partnership shall be published in the paper as is required by law. I, Moses Amos, agree that the $1000.00 One thousand dollars, to be paid after granting charter of Corporation not later than (30) thirty days.

Attest at e
Thos. H. Slater
F. J. Wimberly
Moses Amos

The interior of the Gate City Drug Store. Note the marble tile floor, ceiling lights, and marble counters, c. 1920.

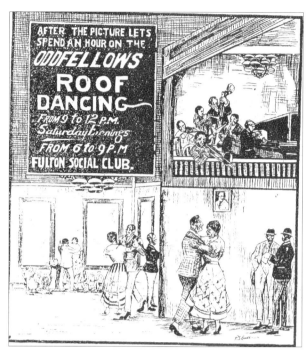

The Auditorium and Armory was the site of numerous performances and sporting events for African-Americans in Atlanta when venues such as the Odd Fellows Auditorium and the Roof Garden on Auburn Avenue could not house the large crowds.

Students at Atlanta University posed in their elegant costumes for one of the numerous Shakespearean performances performed on the picturesque campus, c. 1915–20.

Pupils at the Mitchell Street School, 1915.

Welborn Victor Jenkins and Thomas Jefferson Flanagan were Atlanta's own "negro" poet laureates. They wrote poetry and prose for the Atlanta Independent *and published several books. Jenkins later opened the Beale Laundry on Hunter Street. Flanagan continued to write, serving as editor of* The Scroll *at Atlanta University and writing for the* Atlanta Daily World *for more than forty-five years.*

Members of the Atlanta militia march away from a fire approaching Bedford Pine.

Mount Vernon Baptist Church, founded in 1915, was located near the Terminal Station.

This gentlemen sits in his wagon near Jackson and Angier Avenue amid the destruction of the "great fire" of May 21, 1917, which spread to this part of the Bedford Pine neighborhood.

African-American laborers laying tracks on Peachtree for the trolley cars, c. 1918.

Thousands of African-American men in Atlanta served their country during World War I. In May 1918, hundreds of soldiers and nurses participated in a peace parade through downtown Atlanta to Auburn Avenue and a mass meeting at the First Congregational Church.

This view of Atlanta facing the Flat Iron Building shows one of Alonzo Herndon's barber shops, which extended from Peachtree Street to Broad Street, c. 1918. Besides the large business, note the large signage spelling HERNDON.

Exterior of Herndon's Baths, located next to a vaudeville theater.

Interior of Herndon's Barber Shop

MACKIE BEE HOTEL

The Only Colored Hotel in the City

Electric Lights.   Hot and Cold Baths.   Every Modern Convenience.

Rates $1.00 to $2.00 Per Day

Atlanta has long been in need of a first-class hotel for colored people and the Mackie Bee Hotel meets this need in every respect. It is new, up-to-date and first-class, completely furnished, and meets every requirement of a strictly modern and first-class hotel.

When in Atlanta, stop at the

MACKIE BEE HOTEL

115 Houston Street, Corner Piedmont Avenue

Take the Highland Avenue, or Irwin Street, or Houston Street Car, which will put you off right at the door

MRS. KATIE McBRIDE, Prop.

Formerly of the Martin House

The west side of Butler Street looking north from Baker Street toward Forrest Avenue, 1900s. These rows of homes were occupied by African-Americans.

Sports became an integral part of Atlanta University extracurricular activities. Pictured are the school's basketball and baseball teams on the steps of Stone Hall.

The Herndons

The Wardlaws

The Towns

Chapter 5

A Street Made of Gold, 1920–1929

*T*he whole street was called Negro Peachtree.

Kathleen Redding Adams,
born in 1890 on Auburn Avenue

1920
May. Maj. Robert Russa Moton, principal of Tuskegee Institute, dedicates the Butler Street YMCA.

May. The American Invention Promoting Company, a factory built to market and patent the inventions of African-Americans, opens a $100,000 three-story brick building on Tanner Street, in the old Medical College building near the corner of Edgewood Avenue and Fort Street. Products sold include the Shaw Hairdressing and Manufacturing Chair and the Beasley's Portable Self-Heating Bath Tub. The company encourages African-Americans to buy its stock and pledges to employ thousands of people as traveling and in-house staff.

The first class of the Grady Hospital Training School for "colored" nurses graduates.

More than three hundred African-American students present *The Open Door* at the Auditorium and Armory. The pageant is replete with a symphony and lighting effects.

The Atlanta Branch of the NAACP registers three thousand African-American citizens to help defeat an $8 million bond issue until the city agrees to state how much of the money African-Americans would get for their schools. As a result the African-American community gets $2.5 million, and the following schools are constructed: E. A. Ware, David T. Howard, Yonge Street, Crogman, Walker Street, Ashby Street, and Booker T. Washington High School.

The Atlanta Branch of the NAACP hosts the 22nd annual conference. Participants include Dr. W. E. B. DuBois.

There are 72 African-American businesses and 20 professional offices on Auburn Avenue.

John Hope, president of Morehouse College, helps establish the Atlanta Interracial Commission, an early forerunner to the Southern Regional Conference.

There are 62,796 African-Americans in Atlanta, 31 percent of the total population of 200,000.

The Atlanta City Council creates "racial districts" within the city limits and bars black barbers from serving "white women, white girls, and all white children under fourteen years of age."

Kappa Boule of Sigma Psi Phi, a national business and professional fraternity for African-American males, is chartered.

Leete Hall (now Carver High School) is built on the campus of Clark University (now Clark Atlanta University).

Heman Perry organizes Citizens Trust Company, the second African-American bank in Atlanta.

Fletcher Henderson graduates from Atlanta University. (Henderson later became a renowned band leader.)

1921
February. Mamie Smith and her original Jazz Hounds perform two shows at the Auditorium and Armory. Dubbed the "greatest colored singer of blues in the world," her records are on the OKEH label.

March 10. The cornerstone-laying ceremony for the Auburn Branch Library takes place after a long battle from concerned African-American citizens. Participating are Dr. H. R. Butler, president; John Hope; and Rev. Peter James Bryant. Alice Dugged Cary is the first librarian.

March. Tri-State Big Brother and Big Sister Conference is held by the Atlanta Urban League.

April 26. The Atlanta Urban League presents the Fisk Jubilee Singers at Big Bethel A.M.E. Church.

June 2–4. The Auditorium Theater in the Odd Fellows Annex shows the movie *Youth, Pride, Achievement*, a motion picture of African-Americans in Atlanta.

August 17–19. The Atlanta Branch of the National Negro Business League hosts its national meeting. Over one thousand delegates attend.

August. Construction begins on the new Wheat Street Baptist Church at the corner of Auburn Avenue and Yonge Street. (The church would contain 22 class and department rooms, a vault, and 2,500 seats in the main auditorium. Rev. Peter James Bryant was pastor.)

The Service Company, owned by Heman Perry, begins selling Hunter Street property to African-Americans for the purpose of establishing businesses.

The Beta Chapter of Zeta Phi Beta, the second chapter in its history, is organized at Morris Brown University.

J. E. Jordan starts the Jordan Shop of Quality on the corner of Auburn Avenue and Butler Street.

The East Side Branch of the Citizens Trust Bank opens at 212 Auburn Avenue.

The tenth annual conclave of the Omega Psi Phi fraternity is held in Atlanta at the Butler Street YMCA. Principal speakers include W. J. Trent, Dr. W. F. Penn, and Dr. J. W. E. Bowen.

Heman Perry and Citizens Trust Co.

1921–28 Numerous businesses and establishments are opened on Hunter Street: Parks Shoe Rebuilders (1922), Amos Drug Store (1923), Service Building (1923), West Side Delicatessen (1923), the Crystal Theater (1924), Broadnax Building (1925), and Jenkins Building (1925). Boxer Theodore "Tiger" Flowers purchases two stores and converts them into a restaurant.

1922 July 15. Atlanta's first municipal swimming pool for African-Americans is opened in Washington Park.

October 7. Construction begins for the first public high school for African-Americans in Atlanta.

Heman Perry and the Service Realty Company, after selling land on the West Side to the city for the site of Booker T. Washington High School, begins selling citizens 50' x 100' lots from Ashby Street to C Street (now Whitehouse Drive) and Hunter Street to Beckwith Street. The city also begins racial zoning. (The homes were priced between $3,000 and $8,000 on the average and constructed by "Chief" Walter Aiken's Company, Aiken & Faulkner. Perry also saw to it that the streets were paved.)

A lighted cross and neon lights bearing the words JESUS SAVES are placed on the steeple of Big Bethel A.M.E. Church.

The Phillis Wheatley YWCA launches its first membership drive with a goal of $2,000.

The Mo So Lit Club is organized in the home of Mrs. J. O. Thomas.

1923 February 23. The Atlanta Alumni Chapter of Kappa Alpha Psi is chartered.

Yates and Milton Drug Store opens at the site of the former Gate City Drug Store.

Dr. Moses Amos and his nephew, Dr. Miles Amos, open up the Amos Drug Store on the West Side at the corner of Ashby and Hunter streets.

Sister's Chapel is constructed on the Spelman Seminary campus, providing the largest auditorium facility for the Atlanta University Schools.

The first Boys Club for African-Americans is organized by Marie Finch Simonton.

The Kappa Boule of Sigma Pi Phi fraternity is chartered on January 24 by former Atlantan and Grand Sire Archon Harry H. Pace.

The David T. Howard Grammar School is opened in the Old Fourth Ward.

Antoine Graves, Sr., pioneer African-American realtor, establishes a real estate development on Simpson Road and Ashby Street.

Crisis magazine features the African-American-owned Service Company—a printing, laundry, and dry cleaning establishment; an engineering and construction company; a realty company; and a pharmacy company. Established in 1917 by Heman Perry, its assets are valued at $994,570. The corporation employs 1,600 people.

The Atlanta Interracial Student Forum is organized as an exchange between students from Emory, Morehouse, Spelman, Agnes Scott, Morris Brown, Georgia Tech, Clark, and Atlanta University. Topics include education and accommodations for African-Americans and the student movement in China. The group conducts surveys of Atlanta's hospitals, transportation, housing, and education facilities.

1924

The Paramount, a theater for African-Americans, opens at 92 1/2 Auburn Avenue.

Booker T. Washington High School officially opens with 32 teachers and 1,565 students.

Alonzo Herndon constructs the Herndon Building, an office and hotel facility.

The "27 Club," an organization of married men ranging from 27 to 50 years old, is formed in the home of Dr. Edward G. Bowden. The club's membership is 27, the meetings are held on the 27th of each month, the minimum age is 27, and the meetings begin at 7 minutes after 8:00 P.M.

Spelman Seminary becomes a college.

Graham Jackson begins a three-week stand as a vaudeville performer at the Paramount Theater on Auburn Avenue.

Cascade Heights subdivision is developed. In four days 140 lots are sold, making it one of the largest residential districts open. It is called the Paces Ferry of the southwest side. (Forty years later, African-Americans began to move into the area, causing the mass flight of whites into East Point and Decatur.)

1925

October 15. Madam Lillian Evanti, a famous African-American opera star, performs at the Auditorium and Armory under the auspices of Booker T. Washington High School.

December 18. Roland Hayes sings at the Auditorium.

The third cemetery for African-Americans, Lincoln Memorial Park Cemetery, is established on Simpson Road.

Fifteen men invest $100 each to start Mutual Federal Savings. The founders are J. B. Blayton, Dr. E. G. Bowden, John Wesley Dobbs, C. C. Hart, T. J. Henry, H. M. Ivey, A. M. Carter, W. P. Adams, Charles E. Arnold, Joseph H. B. Evans, T. J. Ferguson, Dr. Charles Johnson, David D. Jones, Dr. T. H. Slater, and J. Garland Woods.

Atlanta police stop Sunday movies at Sunset Amusement Park on the corner of Sunset and Magnolia streets following reports from local African-American ministers. (The ministers argued that "Jews and foreigners who open places where negroes and white folks can meet on terms of social equality should not be permitted to conduct such a nuisance." The park was operated by a Jewish man named Cerf, who agreed not to show any more movies. The case was then dropped.)

Marcus Garvey, known as the "Black Ponzi," arrives in Atlanta to begin serving a five-year prison sentence for mail fraud in connection with his "Back to Africa" Negro colonization project.

1926

The Mozley Park community is annexed to the city of Atlanta.

Harry S. Murphy resigns as vice-president for Standard Life Insurance Company and begins his own printing company, the House of Murphy Printers.

Boxer Theodore "Tiger" Flowers beats Harry Greb and becomes the first African-American to win the middleweight championship.

A replica of the monument of Booker T. Washington at Tuskegee Institute is erected at Booker T. Washington High School.

The Sunset Amusement Park is dubbed "Atlanta's Playground" and is the South's largest "colored" recreation center. It includes a 5,000-foot maplewood dance floor, penny arcade, skee ball alley, merry-go-round, rifle range, theater, boxing arena, and picnic grounds. Bands providing music include the Carver's Famous Orchestra and the Southern Ramblers.

Middleweight boxing champion "Tiger" Flower builds a twenty-room Italian stucco mansion on Simpson Road, two blocks from Ashby Street.

1927   State legislature authorizes racial zoning. (A constitutional amendment supported the decision the following year.)

J. Rosamond Johnson, joint composer of "Lift E'vry Voice and Sing," appears in concert with Taylor Gordon at Big Bethel A.M.E. Church, performing a wide selection of Negro spirituals.

Atlanta University is the first school in the city to install an electric scoreboard.

I. P. Reynolds is named city editor for the *Atlanta Independent.* (Formerly the editor of the *Postal Whip*, Reynolds wrote the column "High Lights of Auburn Avenue" in the *Independent.*)

J. H. and Samuel Sellers establish Sellers Brothers Funeral Home on Hunter Street.

Choruses at Atlanta and Clark Universities record songs on Columbia Records. Atlanta University performs "The Negro National Anthem," and Clark University records "You Shall Have a New Hiding Place."

1928   May 30. The new Carrie Steele Orphanage opens in the Pittsburgh community. Clara Yates is the director.

June. The "Empress of the Blues," Bessie Smith, performs at the 81 Theater.

August 5. The city's second African-American newspaper, the *Atlanta World*, begins publication. It is founded by William A. Scott.

The Church of God in Christ purchases the Crystal Theater on Hunter Street.

Heman Perry's Service Company builds E. A. Ware School on Ashby Street.

William Harris Memorial Hospital is opened by Dr. C. W. Powell on Hunter Street.

Pioneer pharmacist Dr. Moses Amos dies.

Jesse B. Blayton becomes the first African-American certified public accountant in the country.

M. Agnes Jones is supervisor of "colored" public schools.

Twelve-year-old child-prodigy Josephine Harreld, daughter of concert violinist and Morehouse Glee Club director Kemper Harreld, gives a piano recital at the Blue Triangle YMCA.

Graham Jackson opens the West Side Tea Room at 910 West Hunter Street.

Lena Horne moves to Atlanta from Fort Valley, Georgia and resides on C Street (Whitehouse Drive) and attends Booker T. Washington High School. She forms a club with the Blackshear Sisters and they win a dancing prize at the "Kiddie Review" at the Paramount Theater on Auburn Avenue.

1929   Spelman and Morehouse Colleges and Atlanta University organize the Atlanta University System, which includes the Atlanta School of Social Work. They sign an agreement that resources and facilities will be shared.

Oscar Hall and T. L. Curry open the Curry and Hall Style shop, a men's haberdashery on Auburn Avenue.

The four oldest Bronner brothers are employed at the *Atlanta Daily World* as carriers. (The three younger brothers joined them in the mid-1930s.)

Jesse Hanley purchases the Cannon Building on Bell Street and opens Hanley's Funeral Home.

David T. Howard Elementary School becomes a junior high.

The national conference of the NAACP held its convention in Atlanta at Big Bethel A.M.E. Church. Dr. W. E. B. DuBois was one of the keynote speakers, c. 1920.

Charles Walter Hill, first principal of Ashby Street School.

Hattie Landrum Green, second principal, 1919–28.

Bazoline Usher, supervisor of "Negro" schools in Atlanta.

Students in front of the Ashby Street School, c.1921.

Ashby Street School faculty

Storrs School children posed with J. A. Robinson of the Colored Department of the Anti-Tuberculosis Association and Lemuel Foster of the National Urban League. The students were involved in a clean-up campaign for the Tuberculosis Association, c.1921.

Perry's Service Laundry Company had a delivery and pick-up cart pulled by a horse, 1921.

Morris Brown University offered junior high classes on its campus at Houston and Boulevard. The students posed in front of the main academic building, c. 1921.

J. Neal Montgomery (center) is shown with members of his combo. Montgomery played regularly at Bailey's 81 Theater, the Roof Garden, and private socials and dances. He taught at Washington High School but became known throughout Atlanta as a promoter for entertainment acts during the 1930s and 1940s.

Lucius Henderson (right) is shown with an unidentified person in a photographer's studio. Henderson was a partner in the Princess Studio before opening a studio in his home in the Summerhill community.

Shown with his camera, Paul Poole was a veteran photographer who captured through his viewfinder the African-American community of Atlanta in the 1920s and early 1930s.

Ma Rainey, the former Gertrude Pridgett from Columbus, Georgia, established herself as one of the most popular entertainers in the country. She was no stranger to Atlanta audiences, especially the 81 Theater, where she performed throughout the 1910s and 1920s.

The 1920s brought many fraternities and sororities to Atlanta. Pictured are: (1) members of Alpha Phi Alpha Fraternity, Inc. (Eta Lambda Chapter) on the steps of the Atlanta Mutual Association, 1920; (2) the first undergraduate chapter of Delta Sigma Theta at Atlanta University, c. 1922; (3) members of the undergraduate chapter of Alpha Kappa Alpha at Atlanta University, with Mrs. Hilda Evans, adviser and a member of the graduate chapter Kappa Omega, which was established in 1923; and (4) members of the Beta Chapter of Zeta Phi Beta sorority (the second chapter in the nation) at Morris Brown College.

Dr. Edwin Posey Johnson served as pastor of the Reed Street Baptist Church in the Summerhill community for twenty-nine years.

Named for Rev. Edwin P. Johnson, the E. P. Johnson School opened on Martin Street in 1923. It was razed in 1981.

Big Tournament and Prom!!
Come! See the Four Fraternities
Engage in the most Thrilling

Basket Ball Games
OF THE SEASON

At last the Public has what it has been longing for—a thrill-
ing Inter-Fraternity Tournament deciding the "Inter-frat
Champs" followed by the Season's Biggest Hit
A Real Inter-Fraternity Dance

TAFT HALL
AUDITORIUM-ARMORY
SATURDAY
MARCH 6, 1926
Game: 8 P. M.   Dance: 10 P. M.
ADMISSION 35c   COUPLE 50c
GOOD MUSIC
REFRESHMENTS

The Interfraternity Organization of Atlanta sponsored an annual basketball tournament involving members of the four Greek-letter organizations, Alpha Phi Alpha, Kappa Alpha Psi, Omega Psi Phi, and Phi Beta Sigma. In this picture, "Chief" Walter Aiken, well-known contractor and "Omega," coaches the Omega Psi Phi basketball team to the 1926 championship.

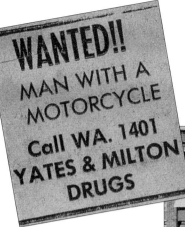

WANTED!!
MAN WITH A
MOTORCYCLE
Call WA. 1401
YATES & MILTON
DRUGS

Professor Charles Lincoln Harper (center) poses with the staff and faculty of the recently opened public high school for African-Americans in Atlanta, named for the late Booker T. Washington, c. 1927.

The Gate City Drug Store was sold to Clayton R. Yates and Lorimer B. Milton in 1922 and renamed Yates and Milton Drug Store.

The Atlanta Life Insurance Company had offices on Auburn Avenue. The columnesque facade was added during the early 1920s.

Alice Dugged Cary (center), the first African-American principal of Morris Brown University, served as the first librarian.

The Auburn Branch Carnegie Library provided African-Americans with quality library services. It opened in 1923.

Football was a revered sport in the African-American community in Atlanta. Shown are (center) the Clark University Panthers, (bottom) the A.U. Crimson and Tide and the Morehouse Tigers battling it out on the Atlanta University field, and (top) the Morris Brown University Wolverines.

A view of homes occupied by African-Americans on Chestnut Avenue, looking east from Piedmont Avenue.

Cox Brothers Funeral home was founded in 1900 by Charles and Allen Cox with their mother, Emily. The funeral cars demonstrate the pride that African-American undertakers took to provide their community with quality funerals, c. 1920s.

Undertaker Jessie Hanley, in a turn-of-the-century buggy, was formerly a magician who established his first funeral home on Edgewood Avenue and later relocated to the building once occupied by George Cannon, founder of Cannolene products on Bell Street.

The first African-American middleweight champion of the world, Theodore "Tiger" Flowers built this home for his wife and daughter on Simpson Road, two blocks west of Ashby Street. The twenty-room Italian stucco mansion featured a training room and butler's quarters. The home was torn down in 1962 for the construction of Firestation No. 16, which housed the first African-American firemen in 1963.

*Dr. G. Waymond
Reeves served as
chairman of the local
Public Health Committee.*

*Dr. J. R. Porter
was a pioneer
dentist in Atlanta.*

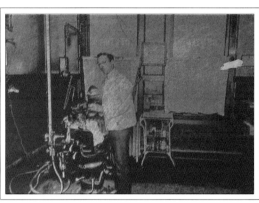

*Dr. Georgia R.
Dwelle may
have been the
first African-
American
female physician
in Atlanta.*

*Dr. Antoine Graves, Jr., former concert violinist, works
on a patient at his office in the Odd Fellows Building
over the Yates and Milton Drug Store at the corner of
Butler Street and Auburn Avenue.*

*Sellers Brothers funeral home was established in 1927 on the west side of Atlanta at 889 Hunter Street by Samuel G.
and J. H. Sellers, who came to Atlanta from Newnan, Georgia. This building was remodeled in 1974, and the entire
front facade was replaced.*

BESSIE SMITH
at **81 THEATRE**
NEXT WEEK

May 1928

*Dr. and Mrs. Henry Rutherford Butler
(Selena Sloan) on an outing. Dr. Butler was
founder of the National Medical Association,
and Mrs. Butler established the Parent-
Teacher Association.*

On stage at the 81 Theater on Decatur Street.

Delivery boys for Munn's Drug Store on Broad Street, 1921.

This fruit and vegetable truck sold fresh produce throughout the African-American community.

Mercy Hospital and Nurse Training School.

When the National Negro Insurance Association met in Atlanta, these hostesses assembled for a convention photo in front of the Atlanta Life Insurance Company.

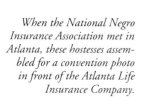

Two children in their front yard, on the corner of Auburn Avenue and Howell Street.

Arthur Trice, a former employee of Judge Garland Watkins, and his wife, Annie, moved from College Park, Georgia, to Atlanta in the mid-1920s and purchased a home on Sunset Avenue in Vine City. Trice became a pullman porter on the Washington-to-New York line. The homes on Sunset had been occupied by white Atlantans before African-Americans began to move into the community. Longstanding families on the street included the Gomillions, Carters, Hightowers, Allens, Howards, Lundys, Cowans, Martins, and Toomers. Later Rev. Maynard H. Jackson, Sr., built a home for his family on the street. Nonye Shepard, a niece of the Trices, referred to Sunset Avenue as the "Pearl of Vine City."

The decade of the twenties in Atlanta closed with the national convention of the Alpha Phi Alpha fraternity meeting in the South for the first time, 1929. According to oral history, during the convention the Ku Klux Klan marched up Auburn Avenue.

Florence Read (president of Spelman College) observes John Hope (president of Morehouse College) sign the agreement establishing the Atlanta University System. Also looking on is Myron Adams (president of Atlanta University).

The display window of the Curry and Hall Style Shop, located on Auburn Avenue. It was one of the few men's shops for African-Americans in Atlanta.

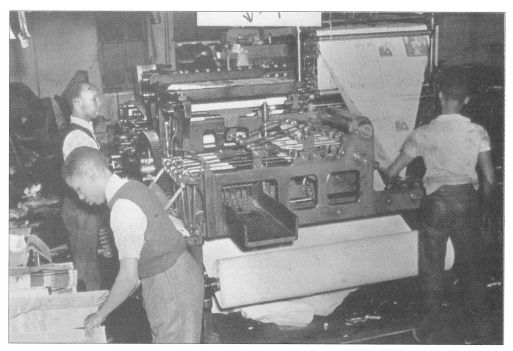

Inside this press plant, the Atlanta World, *the nation's oldest daily newspaper, was printed. Founded in 1928 by William A. Scott, Sr., the* World *was a medium for local, state, national, and international news. Many of the nation's top journalists and photojournalists began their careers with the* Atlanta World *(later the* Atlanta Daily World) *and the Scott syndicated newspapers, including Cliff Mackay, Lerone Bennett, Robert Johnson, and Harmon Perry.*

The Holmes

The Scotts

The Whites

Chapter 6

A Renaissance of the New Negro, 1930–1939

*Self pride and self respect are far more valuable
than the admission of inferiority by going up high
[Negro-only balcony in theaters] to see a $15 show.*

Grace Towns Hamilton

1930 Two African-Americans are arrested for attending a meeting of the American Communist party. (Charged with insurrection laws dating from the 1860s, they eventually were released on bail and left the state.)

Heaven Bound, the story of twenty-four pilgrims trying to reach the heavenly gates, is performed for the first time at Big Bethel A.M.E. Church. (The following year, the theatrical production was performed at the City Auditorium for 6,700 delegates attending the meeting of the Ecumenical Council of Churches. Nellie Davis, Big Bethel chorister, arranged the songs from an idea of Lula Byrd Jones.)

Spelman College discontinues its high school classes and opens a nursery school.

There are 121 African-American businesses and 39 professionals in Atlanta.

Hunter Street is paved and continues to prosper with the addition of the Ashby Theater, Young's Beauty and Barber Shops, the Cannolene Building, the Bethlehem Building, Jack's Shop, Jones's Grocery, Seller Brothers, Jacob's Drug Store, and Evelyn Jones's first restaurant.

The Ku Klux Klan marches down Auburn Avenue to Spelman College (on the west side).

The African-American population in Atlanta climbs to 90,075; the total population of the city is 270,366.

The Order of Black Shirts is founded for the express purpose of driving African-Americans out of jobs and replacing them with whites.

1931 John Norwood and his wife rent a sixty-five-acre farm in the Thomasville section of Atlanta for one bale of cotton per year.

Oscar Hall and Leroy Carter open a service station on Auburn Avenue. The service station will feature Woco Pep gasoline, Purol Ethyl gasoline, and Grayco lubrication.

Sigma Gamma Rho Sorority holds its seventh annual Boule in Atlanta. The Butler Street YMCA is headquarters.

Morris Brown University discontinues its high school and practice school and makes preparation to vacate the campus on Houston and Boulevard. (The university moved to the former Atlanta University campus a year later and changed its name to Morris Brown College.)

A thousand-voice chorus of African-Americans performs to six thousand people attending the National Baptist Convention in Atlanta. George Garner, a native of Georgia, spends a month in Atlanta training the chorus.

John Harden opens a service station on Hunter Street next to the former Church of Christ. (He opened his second station on the Auburn Avenue between Bell and Fort streets in 1935.)

The Atlanta Teachers Federal Credit Union is discussed in the home of Mrs. Oretha Brooks Brown on Linden Street.

African-American artist Hale Woodruff begins teaching art at Atlanta University.

T. M. Alexander opens Alexander and Company, a full-scale insurance company.

1932 January. Citizenship Schools are started at the suggestion of Mrs. John Hope. The school teaches African-Americans how to register to vote in hopes that a white primary eventually would be declared unconstitutional.

January. The musical morality play *Pearly Gates* plays at the City Auditorium and features the Morris Brown Symphony Orchestra under the direction of Earl A. Starling.

February 11. Nationally renowned tenor Roland Hayes, a native of Georgia who has sung for the king and queen of England, performs at the Wesley Memorial Church. Tickets are

$2.00, $1.50, and $1.00 and are sold at Yates and Milton Drug Store.

March. At a banquet at the James Hotel in the Herndon Building on Auburn Avenue, publisher W. A. Scott II announces that the *Atlanta World* will become a daily newspaper.

August. The Atlanta Negro Chamber of Commerce is organized.

September 12. Tom Finch, an African-American orderly at Grady Hospital, is shot five times by a "mob" that "arrested" him for an alleged crime.

The African-American community rallies behind Mayor John Key in a recall election.

Thousands of unemployed workers, including African-Americans, march on the courthouse protesting the inadequacy of city relief measures.

The first African-American family to move to Angier Avenue is the Miller family. Whites leave the Bedford Pine community in a mass exodus.

Angelo Herndon, a nineteen-year-old African-American, is arrested by Atlanta police and accused of violating Georgia's notorious sedition law, which consists of distributing Communist literature to destitute families, and arranging meetings and making speeches in the name of the Communist Party of America.

Otis and E. A. Pollard open Pollard Funeral Home in an old house on Fraser Street in the Summerhill community.

Atlanta native and actor Daniel Hayes returns to Harlem after forty-eight weeks on the road in the traveling version of *The Green Pastures.* He stars in the role of Adam.

1933 John Hope, president of Morehouse College, is contacted by the National Real Estate Board, about a possible slum clearance project in the Beaver Slide area. Hope goes to Washington, D.C., and pleads the cause before the Works Progress Administration (WPA). (A year later, Harold L. Ickes, secretary of the Interior, came to Atlanta to dynamite the first home in Beaver Slide.)

Lorimer Milton, Clayton Yates, and Jesse Blayton purchase the stock of Citizens Trust Bank and reorganize.

John Wesley Dobbs is elected the grand master of the Prince Hall Masonic Lodge of Georgia.

Entertainer "Fats" Waller performs at the City Auditorium.

John Harden opens his third service station on the corner of Simpson and Chestnut streets.

1934 John Wesley Dobbs organizes the Atlanta Civic and Political League.

Eric "Ric" Roberts, journalist for the *Atlanta Daily World,* asks in a column, "Who will be the wrongest guy?" and the 100% Wrong Club is born. (Thirteen sports enthusiasts responded and became the founders of the club: C. R. Higginbotham, T. Shelton Coles, Jimmy Perry, Hubert Jackson, W. A. Hamilton, A. T. Hollingsworth, Michael Turrentine, J. C. Chunn, Lucius Jones, Joel Smith, Bacharach Smith, and LeRoy Carter.)

February. An African-American man posing as a prophet, claiming to be a descendant of the pharaohs of Egypt, attracts attention on the corner of Auburn Avenue and Butler Street.

A standing-room-only, overflowing crowd packs the Sunset Casino to watch the world-renowned New York Rens basketball team from Harlem defeat "Chief" Walter Aikens's All-Stars. The All-Stars are Leroy NcNeil, Frank DeCosta, Carl Ray, and H. Archer.

The Apex Beauty College opens. Mrs. Louise Williams Hollowell is director. (The school was located on the corner of Auburn Avenue and Butler Street before it moved to the Prince Hall Masonic Building at 330 Auburn Avenue.)

Cornelius King, Sr., dies.

During the performance of *Heaven Bound* at the Municipal Auditorium, a part of the stage crashes, injuring several people. (It was then decided that the pageant would be produced only in the Big Bethel sanctuary. The musical had become an annual event, playing to over-flow audiences on Friday and Saturday nights in November.)

A full-page ad in the *Atlanta Daily World* congratulates Citizens Trust Bank for being accepted into the Federal Deposit Insurance Corporation.

John Wesley Dobbs, railroad mail clerk and civic leader, organizes the Atlanta Civic and Political League to encourage African-Americans to become involved in the political process.

Interracial mass meetings protesting the inequitable distribution of relief take place at the state capitol each month.

W. A. Scott II, founder of the *Atlanta Daily World*, is killed.

1935   April 16. David T. Howard dies.

Fred D. Maise, owner of Maise's Department Store on the corner of Auburn Avenue and Butler Street, unveils his newly decorated store with a "ready to wear line" and nationally known Kinney brand of shoes.

Rev. Martin Luther King, Sr., leads a voter-registration march on city hall.

The *Atlanta Daily World* begins its Christmas Cheer program.

1936   The Phillis Wheatley Branch YWCA moves to 218 Boulevard.

The Roof Garden at the Odd Fellows Building is destroyed by a fire. (It housed the Club Royale.)

African-American teachers begin meeting to discuss discriminatory pay scales.

John Calhoun opens the Calhoun Furniture Shop on Auburn Avenue.

William Calloway opens the Calloway Realty Company on Auburn Avenue.

1937   Miss R. E. Pruden is the first African-American woman to take the state law examination in the Fulton County Courthouse.

The family of the late Cornelius King presents a public-address system to Big Bethel A.M.E. Church. (The church's minister, Rev. D. T. Babcock, had asked for such a gift because of the numerous requests to hold cultural events and political meetings there. Big Bethel was one of the most-used facilities of African-Americans in the city.)

The WPA presents *Heaven Bound* at the Atlanta Federal Theater.

The 15th Grand Boule of the Sigma Pi Phi fraternity meets in Atlanta. Archon A. T. Walden expresses belief that "Atlanta with its business, schools and universities pointed the way to things cultural."

The 23rd Annual Grand Conclave of the Omega Psi Phi fraternity and the 21st Annual Conclave of the Phi Beta Sigma fraternity are held simultaneously in Atlanta, bringing the largest contingency of African-American men to the city at one time.

Mrs. C. M. Pearson opens the Savoy Hotel in the Herndon Building, following the closing of the James Hotel. Hundreds of people come to see the Savoy sign light up on Auburn Avenue. (The Savoy Hotel Ballroom staged regular dances every Saturday and Monday, with the Jones and Brown Orchestra providing music.)

The first graduation of Poro College is held at Big Bethel A.M.E. Church. A banquet is held at Ma Sutton's Restaurant with over 125 in attendance. C. L. Harper is toastmaster. Ella Martin Ramsey, president of the college, is very active in the community. She becomes the first woman since Reconstruction to run for a seat in the House of Representatives on the Republican ticket and is invited by Governor Herman Talmadge to bring beauticians to the legislature to speak on a bill affecting the profession.

John Wesley Dobbs organizes the Atlanta Negro Voters League.

University Homes, offering public housing for African-American residents, opens.

Ella Fitzgerald performs in Atlanta for the first time, at the Sunset Casino with the Chick Webb Orchestra. Admission is 65 cents.

Guy Miller opens the Atlanta College of Embalming on the corner of Chestnut and Hunter streets. It is one of the few African-American-owned and -operated mortuary schools in the country.

Jesse B. Blayton, Clayton R. Yates, and Lorimer D. Milton open the Top Hat Club on Auburn Avenue. Plumbing is installed by African-American plumber C. C. Hart.

1938   Jackson's Appliances, the first African-American-owned and -operated appliance store is opened by Menelik Jackson and his wife, Ethelda, in the Herndon Building.

Evelyn Jones opens the Chicamauga Café and later the Evelyn Jones Café on Hunter Street. (In 1940, she married Luther Frazier, who helped her with the business.)

1939   Matthew Simpson Davage, president of Clark University, speaks before the all-white Atlanta Rotary Club. However, he is not allowed to eat with them. The title of his speech is "The Negro's Place in Atlanta's Life."

Ebenezer Baptist Church Choir No. 2, dressed in plantation costumes, performs at the premier of *Gone With the Wind*, at Lowe's Grand Theater.

Charles L. Harper Field is dedicated.

Alfred "Tup" Holmes, son of Dr. Hamilton M. Holmes, competes in the National Intercollegiate Golf Tournament in Des Moines, Iowa. His participation breaks the racial barrier in this tournament.

The Baptist World Alliance meets at the Savoy Hotel.

Ten African-American women principals charter the Atlanta Teachers Credit Union. They are: M. Agnes Jones (Houston Street), Cora B. Finley (Yonge Street), Bessie E. Smith (Ashby Street), Hattie Landrum Green (Gray Street), Rachel O'Neal Brown (Summerhill), Nellie L. Barber (Bell Street), Mary Cook Barber (E. A. Ware), Carrie B. Pittman (Crognam), Lena Campbell (South Atlanta), and Jessie Mae Jones (E. A. Ware).

The Atlanta College of Embalming and Mortuary Science opens at the corner of Chestnut and Hunter streets. Guy L. Miller is president, and Burrell T. Harvey is dean.

SINCERE GREETINGS

BAILEY
THEATRES

Eighty-One – Royal – Ashby
Lincoln – Harlem – Strand

Decatur Street was full of small businesses, including restaurants, loan shops, groceries, and clothing and hardware stores, many of which were owned and operated by African-Americans. It was the second largest major thoroughfare for African-Americans in Atlanta. The street was also laden with speakeasies, bars, prostitution, and gambling, and thus dubbed the "Red Light" district.

The most popular building on Decatur Street was Bailey's 81 Theater, which was opened in 1910 by Charles P. and Flora Bailey. As Atlanta's legitimate vaudeville theater and picture show for African-Americans, the theater had an orchestra pit where many of Atlanta's prominent musicians—among them Eddie Heywood, Sr.; Eddie Heywood, Jr.; J. Neal Montgomery; and Graham Jackson—got their start with the house band. Entertainers such as Butter Bean and Susie, Ethel Waters, the Whitman Sisters, Bessie Smith, and Ma Rainey also performed there. In 1923, the 81 Theater presented Noble Sissle and Eubie Blake's broadway musical Shuffle Along, *straight from New York. In later years a young singer from Macon, Georgia, named Richard Penniman, won a talent show at the 81. He would later be known as "Little Richard." The landmark theater closed in the 1960s and was razed. Currently, the Georgia State University Library occupies the block on Decatur Street where the theater once stood.*

Blues guitarist Blind Willie McTell

The Lincoln Country Club was chartered in 1930 by Alonzo Fisher, James Ivey, Theodore Grimes, and A. W. Parks and would be the site of numerous social functions. Introducing the sport of golf on a larger scale to the African-American community in Atlanta, Fisher constructed a 33–acre nine-hole golf course in a highly secluded, wooded area on Simpson Road. In 1937, after the devastating Great Depression, the club was reorganized as the New Lincoln Country Club. New charter members included Dr. Hamilton M. Holmes, W. H. Wheeler, Fred A. Toomer, A. H. Chatman, J. E. Williams, Joel Smith, and Mel Moye. The building burned in the late 1980s, and Lincoln Cemetery acquired the property to expand its burial grounds.

STUDENTS AND FACULTY OF THE ATLANTA UNIVERSITY
LABORATORY ELEMENTARY SCHOOL — (OGLETHORPE)
W.A ROBINSON-PRINCIPAL
(MAY-18-1932)
PHOTO BY KELLY

er-Treasurer | J. H. HANLEY, Pres., and Owner, | S. W. WALKER, V. Pres. Dist. Mgr | C. R. YATES, Managing Partner | J. E. JORDAN, President, | W. A. SCO
t Co. | The Hanley Company | Pilgrims Health and Life Ins. Co. | Yates and Milton Pharmacy | Jordan's Shop Of-Quality, Inc. | T

Cliff Mackay joined the staff of the Atlanta Daily World *in the 1931 as a photojournalist. He later became managing editor and worked until 1945 before going to the* Afro-American. *While in Atlanta, Mackay conducted a campaign against the high Atlanta homicide rate and rallied for industrial training for African-Americans.*

After the murder of W. A. Scott II, founder of the Atlanta Daily World *in 1934, his brother Cornelius A. Scott assumed leadership of the nation's only African-American daily newspaper.*

Professor Henry Furlow, teacher at David T. Howard High School, served as director of the Big Bethel Church Choir and was most noted for his portrayal of the devil in the annual presentation of Heaven Bound, *a theatrical production on spiritual morality and good versus evil. The event still attracts a large contingency of white Atlantans to the church on Auburn Avenue for this annual holiday tradition.*

Interior of Big Bethel A.M.E. Church, where Rev. D. T. Babock served as pastor.

African-American scouting in Atlanta used proven methods to train young men to be responsible and productive citizens. Churches such as Friendship Baptist, First Congregational, and Ebenezer sponsored troops and attracted not only members of the congregation but also other neighborhood boys. Andrew Jackson Lewis served as one of the pioneering leaders of scouting in Atlanta.

One of the WPA projects for the blind was in an unidentified church on Bankhead Highway.

Health care in Atlanta for African-Americans during the 1930s emphasized the education and treatment of tuberculosis. Physicians both black and white were kept abreast of studies and treatment of the disease. Note the racial separation of the doctors. The African-American doctors pictured behind the standing white doctor are (l–r) Dr. Homer E. Nash, Dr. Jackson, and Dr. Hamilton Holmes.

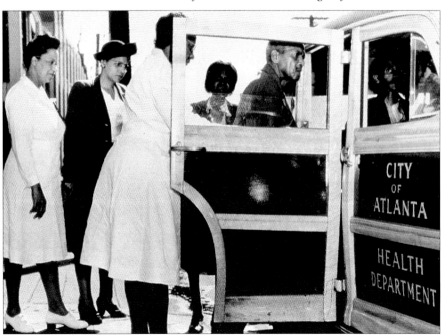

Elderly citizens being transported by the City of Atlanta Health Department for public health-care needs.

*This African-American woman is
being examined for tuberculosis
during "Negro" Health Week.*

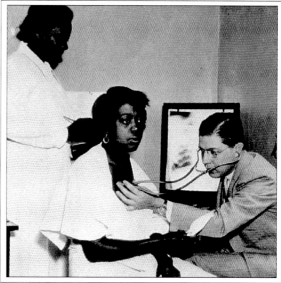

David T. Howard Junior High School, faculty basketball team, 1932.

A panoramic view from southwest Atlanta. To the far left is the campus of Morehouse College and to the far right is Atlanta University (Morris Brown College). These houses were replaced by the university and John Hope Homes Federal Housing Project, c. 1935.

This home on Boulevard was designed and constructed by Aiken & Faulkner and was the residence of several prominent African-American families in Atlanta, including the Hamilton-Holmes family. For more than twenty-five years, Rev. William A. Fountain, bishop of the A.M.E. church and president of Morris Brown College, lived with his family there. The home featured a solarium, winding stairs, and an exterior wall of glass overlooking the city. According to oral history, the home was a "love gift" for a racially mixed couple who were forced to leave the structure. It just barely missed being razed by the construction of an Interstate 75/85 exit ramp.

Commitment Service at the grave of Dr. John Hope, president of Morehouse College and Atlanta University.

Looking north of Atlanta from the Summerhill area. The homes surrounding the state capitol were demolished and replaced by government buildings and, to the right, the Interstate Highway, c. 1936.

Ma Sutton's Restaurant on Auburn Avenue was a frequent spot for banquets and dinners sponsored by African-American businesses, clubs, and organizations. The restaurant, opened in 1920, was torn down during the construction of the interstate overpass, which wiped out several blocks of businesses owned by African-Americans.

A spectacular fire destroyed the Club Royal, on top of the seven-story Odd Fellows Building at the corner of Auburn Avenue and Bell Street. Patrons attending the Royal Theater filed out safely, avoiding injury, c. 1936.

Before the term "movers and shakers" became common, the African-American community could count on these men to "shake" things up in the name of progress: (l–r) 1st row, R. E. Cureton, John Whittaker, and C. C. Hart; 2nd row, Gilbert "Grit" DeLorme, Norris B. Herndon, Walter Smith, and Frederick Brooks; 3rd row, William S. Cannon, Eugene M. Martin, and unidentified; 4th row, Reverend Strong, unidentified, and John Wesley Dobbs. They were all members of the Covenant Club of the First Congregational Church.

Tennis became a popular sport for African-Americans in Atlanta during the 1930s.

Lugenia Burns Hope, wife of Dr. John Hope (1st row, 2nd from right), at the meeting of the National Women's Council in Washington, D.C.

Wash day at the rear of a home on Davis Street (now Northside Drive), c. 1939.

This aerial view of northeast Atlanta shows the vast amount of African-American housing that would be replaced by federal housing and named Henry Grady Homes, c. 1939.

House facing Gilmer Street, 1939.

Moving from a house on Davis Street, c. 1939.

Junction of Larkin Street, Greensferry Avenue, and Chapel Street, c. 1939.

Looking southwest on Peters Street. The upstairs of this store-front housed several African-American families, c. 1939.

Corner of Decatur and Bell streets, c. 1939.

1937

Jesse B. Blayton, Clayton R. Yates, and Lorimer Milton organized a corporation known as BLMIYA, which in 1937 opened the Top Hat Club on Auburn Avenue. Known as "Club Beautiful," the Top Hat was considered one of the finest clubs for African-Americans in the country.

Martin and Mable Hawk opened Hawk's Dinette on Auburn Avenue. It immediately became a popular spot for dining. A slice of homemade pie was served with each meal, c. 1938.

The 1939 graduating class of the APEX Beauty College included one male, Nathaniel Bronner, who later founded Bronner Brother Beauty Supply.

An unidentified truckload of children in front of Stone Mountain.

Chapter 7

"A Voteless People Is a Hopeless People," 1940–1949

*G*et the ballot and the dollar and
you'll walk in Jerusalem just like John.

John Wesley Dobbs

1940   The John Hope Homes, which replace 500 slum dwellings with 606 apartments, opens.

Atlanta's African-American population is 104,533, 33 percent of the total population of 302,288.

The NAACP continues to fight to remove the ban on African-American teachers holding positions after marriage, effective protest against police brutality, and petitions for the equalization of teachers' salaries.

The Atlanta Chapter of the National Beauty Culturist League is organized. (The twenty-second annual session of the league met at the Butler Street YMCA the following year.)

Forty percent of the African-American population has moved to the west side. Efforts to expand to Ashby Street, north of Simpson along English Avenue, is met with home burnings and threats.

Charles Lincoln Harper is elected president of the Georgia Teachers and Education Association.

Dr. Horace Mann Bond speaks to six hundred youths at a youth conference at Friendship Baptist Church.

The Atlanta Charitable Educational and Festival Association sponsors an outing for African-Americans at the Lakewood Park. Admission is 25 cents.

C. L. Harper

1941   Four New Deal housing projects—Grady, Eagan, Herndon, and Capitol Homes—are completed, bringing a total of eight federally funded housing projects.

Holsey Temple, C.M.E. Church, one of the oldest "Colored Methodist Episcopal" churches in Atlanta, pays off its eighteen-year debt of $6,000. A bus is purchased to accommodate Sunday School students living in the remote sections of the city and elderly people who find it uncomfortable to ride the streetcar.

Bandleader Fletcher Henderson returns home to perform at the Top Hat Club with his orchestra. (Fletcher graduated from Atlanta University in 1920 and went off to New York to pursue his music career.)

Vibraphonist Lionel Hampton performs at the City Auditorium.

Charles L. Harper and other African-American educators meet with Governor Eugene Talmadge in 1941 and urge him to use his "Official Power" to better the financial status of African-American teachers and to provide state aid for graduate and professional study for African-American youth of Georgia.

Fletcher Henderson

Eddie Heywood, former Atlanta pianist and bandleader and father of Lottie Heywood Watkins, records with Billie Holliday.

The Atlanta Branch of the NAACP investigates a brutality case involving the alleged slapping, choking, and beating of a female student at Booker T. Washington High School in downtown Atlanta by a white couple. It is also mounting a campaign for Ruth Thornton, who was kicked in the mouth by a white man when both attempted to enter a streetcar at the same time.

Atlanta University begins its annual exhibition of paintings, sculptures, and prints by "Negro artists."

1942   The Atlanta Civic and Political League urges all registered voters to stay away from the polls to issue a negative response against a house issue for which only $100,000 will be allocated to "Negro" schools.

The Washington Aircraft School opens to teach African-Americans in Atlanta aircraft work.

A petition is filed in the U.S. District Court by William H. Leeven, a teacher at David T. Howard High School, asking that African-American schoolteachers be paid the same salaries as white teachers. The case is being represented by attorneys A. T. Walden and Thurgood Marshall, legal representative of the NAACP.

1943

Grace Towns Hamilton is appointed director of the Atlanta Urban League.

A biracial committee adopts a resolution establishing the Southern Regional Council.

The Atlanta Urban League publishes "The Negro School Child in Atlanta." Out of 70,894 school-age children, the pamphlet reports, 26,528 are African-Americans, for which there are only 13 public school buildings and for which only $37.80 is spent per child as compared to $108.70 spent for white students.

Alexander-Calloway Realty Company is established. William L. Calloway is president.

A survey is published on African-American businesses in Atlanta.

1944

December. The *American Front* magazine, a publication for "American people with hopes and aspirations," debuts. It is edited and published by Percy E. Johnson, on Drummond Street in southwest Atlanta.

Bailey's Royal Theater opens in the Odd Fellows Annex Auditorium, which seats 1,300 people.

African-Americans attempt to vote in Georgia's all-white primary.

The Westside Health Center, the first public health center for African-Americans in Georgia, opens.

A petition is submitted to Mayor William B. Hartsfield for the widening of Magnolia Street from Davis Street to Chestnut Street and for Sunset Avenue from Magnolia to Hunter Street to be improved. Travel could then be facilitated from Simpson south to Hunter Street, relieving traffic on other parallel streets.

Atlanta's own cinematographer and photographer, J. Richardson Jones, produces a film for the Atlanta Negro Chamber of Commerce entitled *Parade of Negro Progress.*

Benjamin J. Davis, Jr., and Rev. Adam Clayton Powell, Jr., are invited to participate in the planning of an Atlanta "Town Hall" for the African-American community.

The *Atlanta Daily World* initiates a mass voter-registration drive. (At the time African-Americans had to pay a dollar registration fee.)

1945

September. Chimes are installed at Wheat Street Baptist Church and are played both inside and outside every Saturday evening and Sunday morning. (An African-American electrical technician, Edward C. Wilson, did the installation.)

October. Mahalia Jackson, gospel singer, and Thomas A. Dorsey, gospel singer, writer, and composer, appear in concert at the Zion Hill Baptist Church at the corner of McDaniel Street and Georgia Avenue. Admission is 25 cents.

The Hungry Club Forum is organized. Meetings are held at the Butler Street YMCA. The club's motto is "Food for Taste and Food for Thought for Those Who Hunger for Information and Association."

Clark College opens three new buildings on its new campus: Merner Hall, Thayer Hall, and Pfeiffer Hall.

Sam Carroll's Dew Drop Inn opens at 11 Ashby Street.

The first African-American kindergarten opens.

The Butler Street YMCA

Herschel Thornton opens Thornton Funeral Home at 843 Mitchell Street.

(He relocated to southwest Atlanta in 1964.)

Hundreds of African-American citizens protest in front of City Hall demanding that the city hire African-American policemen.

Mary McLeod Bethune speaks at Wheat Street Baptist Church in a program sponsored by the Atlanta Metropolitan Council of Negro Women, an affiliate of the National Council of Negro Women.

The Nicholas Brothers dancing team appears with Dizzy Gillespie and his orchestra at the City Auditorium.

April. A candlelight service is held at the City Auditorium in conjunction with the All Citizens Registration Committee, which was the largest campaign to register African-Americans to vote.

James and Robert Paschal open a lunchroom on Hunter Street specializing in chicken sandwiches.

The Evelyn Jones Café is renamed Frazier's Café Society and features the Graham Jackson room for banquets and parties.

Dr. F. Earl McLendon opens the McLendon Medical Clinic on the west side at the corner of Sharon Street and Chicamauga Avenue.

Evelyn Jones Frazier, owner of Frazier's Café Society.

A massive voter-registration drive aimed at African-Americans is organized by the NAACP, the newly formed All Citizens Registration Committee, and other organizations. A total of 24,137 African-Americans register.

Rev. William Holmes Borders heads the first major Public Defenders Project in which over $10,000 is raised to defend victims of racial reprisal in Monroe, Georgia.

Auburn Avenue, as part of an urban renewal project, is subject to be bought up by the Atlanta Housing Authority for resale to businesses or individuals. *Atlanta Daily World's* Cornelius A. Scott and others take the lead in convincing the city to leave Auburn Avenue out of the urban renewal area.

The Association for the Study of Negro Life and History meets in Atlanta on the campus of Atlanta University. Conference participants include Mary McLeod Bethune; Dr. Rayford Logan, chair of the Howard University history department; and Dr. Charles Harris Wesley, president of Wilberforce University. Dr. Clarence A. Bacote, chair of the Atlanta University history department, is host.

Joe Cox, proprietor of the Bowliseum Sandwich Bar, opens Joe's Coffee Bar on Auburn Avenue.

Singer Big Maybelle begins her music career in Atlanta singing with the Red McAllister band for two years. (She was known for the songs "Candy" and "Mean to Me.")

1947 June 15–21. The National Association of Colored Graduate Nurses meets in Atlanta.

December 1. The Atlanta City Council approves the hiring of African-American policemen. However, the police union wins a stay order, preventing action on the council's ruling.

The Phillis Wheatley Branch YWCA purchases 118 acres of land in Newnan, Georgia, and establishes Camp Ida Prather.

The Atlanta Urban League publishes "A Report on Hospital Care of the Negro Population of Atlanta, Georgia" and sets off a five-year effort to improve health and hospital care to African-Americans.

Nathaniel, Clinton, and Arthur Bronner open up Bronner Brothers Beauty and Hair Products on the corner of Auburn Avenue and Butler Street with $1,000.

John Wesley Dobbs and Austin T. Walden organize the Atlanta Negro Voter League.

Congress grants a press card to a reporter from the *Atlanta Daily World*.

Brown Boy Bottling Company is purchased and operated by BLMIYA, Inc., an acronym of Blayton, Milton and Yates.

The Calhoun Street School is converted to a school for African-Americans. The name is changed to the C. W. Hill Elementary School in honor of Charles Walter Hill, a pioneer African-American elementary school principal. The new principal is Ms. Nell Hamilton, and the school opens with 2,500 students from grades one to seven.

The What-Knots Social Club is organized by Mattie Harden and Maude Lakes.

The George Washington Carver Boys Club is dedicated at 481 Thurmond Street. John Wesley Dobbs is chair of the Colored Division.

David T. Howard Junior High becomes Atlanta's second high school for African-Americans.

James and Robert Paschal expand their lunchroom into a restaurant at 837 Hunter Street with three employees and a seating capacity of thirty.

1948

February 26. The police union's stay is overturned.

April 3. Eight men become Atlanta's first African-American policemen. They are stationed in the basement of the Butler Street YMCA and cannot arrest white citizens.

December 19. A report on the effects of separate school systems is issued by the Atlanta Urban League. According to the report, African-Americans live in areas that contain 72 percent of the city's juvenile delinquency, 60 percent of its crime, and 69 percent of its tuberculosis cases.

The Catholic Archdiocese of Atlanta Our Lady of Lourdes Mission starts the Catholic Colored Peoples Clinic at 348 Forrest Avenue. It is run by nuns and James J. Grady, who uses an old station wagon to transport patients.

The Gate City Bar Association is founded. (African-Americans were excluded from the Atlanta Bar Association.)

Literary artist J. Saunders Redding, author of *No Day of Triumph*, speaks to Atlanta University Center students.

Newly installed police officers stand at ease outside their precinct station at the Butler Street YMCA as W. A. Scott takes their picture, c. 1948.

1949

October. "Strictly for Lovers," a daily radio program presented on WERD by well-known local dramatist Raphael McIver, consists of love poems read with a background of enchanting music. His programs include "Morning Meditation."

Jesse Hill, after graduating from Lincoln University and the University of Michigan, moves to Atlanta and resides in the Butler Street YMCA. He joins the staff of Atlanta Life Insurance Company. (In 1977 he became the third president of the company.)

The Atlanta Negro Voters League is organized by John Wesley Dobbs and Austin T. Walden.

The David T. Howard High School publishes the first edition of the school's yearbook, *The Ram*.

A football stadium is constructed on the campus of Morris Brown College through the generosity of Norris B. Herndon, president of Atlanta Life Insurance Company. The stadium is named the Alonzo Herndon Memorial Stadium.

Mayor William Hartsfield is reelected as African-Americans participate in the first mayoral primary since the white primary was declared unconstitutional.

Jesse Blayton purchases WERD Radio Station, becoming the first African-American radio station owner in the country. It begins broadcasting on October 7.

Rev. W. W. Weatherspool and his family purchase a home in the Mozley Park neighborhood. (The purchase sparked a controversy involving Governor Herman Talmadge, Mayor

William Hartsfield, C. A. Scott of the *Atlanta Daily World*, Charles L. Harper of the NAACP, and others. Within five years the entire Mozley Park area would shift from white to African-American.)

Police cars are provided to the Atlanta's African-American policemen for patrolling their beat.

Mrs. Thrasher Davis, a former slave of John Thrasher who recalled playing on the land that is now the Georgia State Capitol, dies at the Old People's Nursery Home at the age of 112.

WERD staff personnel include Raphael McIver, Johnny Martin, Dave Bondu, Joe Starr, Bob Brisendine, Graham Jackson, Jack Gibson, B. T. Harvey, and Mrs. Billie Geter Thomas. The *Atlanta Daily World* will offer forty-five minutes of on-the-air news scattered throughout the day.

The Royal Peacock (formerly the Top Hat Club) opens with performers Annie Laurie, Paul Gayten, a chorus of girls, exotic dancers, and the Tyler and Tyler dance team. Red McAllister is manager. Admission is $1.00. Tickets can be purchased at Paschal Brothers and Zack's Smoke House.

Bailey Theater opens up the Carver Theater on the corner of McDonough Boulevard and Jonesboro Road. Other businesses recently developed in the same block include a laundry, dry-cleaning store, five-and-ten-cents store, and poultry and grocery market. This business development is a welcome addition to the south Atlanta community.

The Negro Branch Library is renamed the Library Service Department as the West Hunter Branch is opened.

W. A. Scott III, son of the founder of the Atlanta Daily World. *A photojournalist, Scott sent the* World *photographs of Nazi concentration camps during World War II.*

Editor C. A. Scott and businessman Jesse B. Blayton talk to Oscar S. De Priest, Sr., the first African-American U.S. congressman from Illinois, in front of the Atlanta Daily World *office.*

Aerial view of the area that would later occupy the Alonzo Franklin Herndon Public Housing projects, c. 1940.

Holsey Temple, C.M.E. Church, one of the oldest "Colored Methodist Episcopal" churches in Atlanta, pays off its eighteen-year debt of $6,000. A bus is purchased to accommodate Sunday School students living in the remote sections of the city and elderly people who find it uncomfortable to ride the street-car.

Gwendolyn Cooper, daughter of well-known dentist Dr. Albert Cooper, walks up the driveway of their home on picturesque Hunter Street. The residential portion of Hunter Street featured paved sidewalks, beautiful shrubbery, and trees and demonstrated the middle-class life of African-Americans in Atlanta. Note the birdfeeder in the tree.

These two homes represent the affluence of the block of Auburn Avenue between Jackson and Howell streets. Later the Negro Culture League, founded by Ruby Blackburn, occupied one of the homes.

Inside of Amos Drug Store, where, according to Atlanta lore, "the best hot dogs and malts were sold."

Amos Drug Store opened in 1923 on the corner of Ashby and Hunter streets.

Bishop K. H. Burruss, the moving spirit and inspiration of the Churches of God Holiness, led the congregation at the Bethlehem Church of God on Hunter Street, in the former Crystal Theater building.

The Booker T. Washington High School Marching Band under the direction of Earl Starling.

Booker T. Washington High School, 1941.

The 1942 graduating class of Booker T. Washington High School.

Classical singer Marian Anderson (left) is accompanied by Florence Read, president of Spelman College, as she leaves a performance on the campus, 1941.

Atlanta University was a welcome mat for distinguished educators, scholars, and celebrities during the 1940s. Pictured is Dr. E. Franklin Frazier (2nd from left), former director of the Atlanta School of Social Work, who returned for a lecture. Flanking him (l–r) are Walter Chivers, Dr. W. E. B. DuBois, and Dr. Ira D. Reid.

Paul Robeson speaks before a delegation at Sister's Chapel on the Spelman College campus. He served as commencement speaker for Morehouse College in 1940.

The Morehouse College football team.

This group of friends and members of a Spelman graduating class were guests of honor at a dance sponsored by their parents at the Top Hat Club.

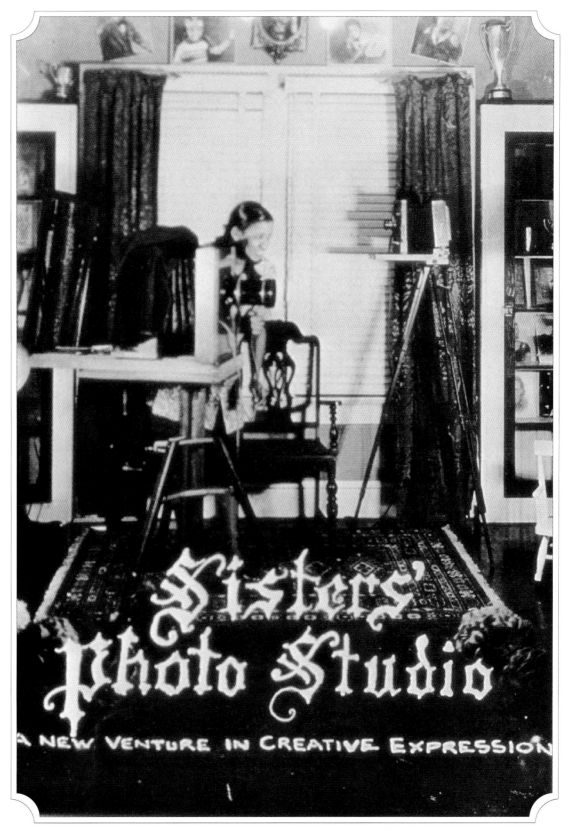

Ruth Hall Hodges was the first African-American woman in Atlanta to own a photography studio. Her Sisters Photo Studio was located on Ashby Street. Dr. Hodges taught art at Morris Brown College, and, to raise money for the art department, she sponsored Little Miss Morris Brown pageants. One of her contestants included little Gladys Knight.

Mr. S. W. Walker (standing on right end), founder of Pilgrim Life Insurance Company in Augusta, with members of the Reed Street Baptist Church Mother's Board in the Summerhill community, where he resided.

Program for Poro's School of Atlanta, June 16, 1942.

The delivery truck of Bronner Brothers Beauty Supply Company. The company offices were located at the corner of Butler Street and Auburn Avenue.

James E. Jordan, "the Black Jew of Auburn Avenue," founded Hy Beaute Products and was a cinematographer and photographer.

This accident, in which a streetcar hit a young man, blocked traffic on Auburn Avenue. The Irwin Street trolley and other cars had to wait for the Murdaugh Brothers hearse, which came to pick up the injured man, to move. The man survived the accident.

The Smoke House on Auburn Avenue sold a variety of cigars and other tobacco products and offered "spit" shines for shoes.

Andrew Taylor Kelly, "the Dean of Black Photographers in Atlanta," operated studios on Auburn Avenue and Chestnut and Fair streets for more than forty years.

Jackson Appliance Store featured unique window displays. This display focuses on "The Negro in Books." The store was located in the Herndon Building and was the first African-American-owned store of its kind in Atlanta.

The Chita-Chata Restaurant, located on Simpson Road, was billed as "The South's Finest Colored Drive-In," c. 1949.

Standing in the middle is the legendary Geneva Moton Haugabrooks, owner of Haugabrooks Funeral Home and one of the most well-known women in Atlanta. A former schoolteacher and cook for Georgia governor John M. Slaton, she established her funeral business in 1929 on Auburn Avenue. It later moved to its present location, 364 Auburn Avenue.

The original O. S. Hall Service Station on Auburn Avenue, pictured here, was torn down and rebuilt in the 1960s.

Not only had Simpson Road businesses developed by the 1940s but also its residential areas. Dr. and Mrs. P. Q. Yancey and family were some of the first African-Americans to build homes on Simpson Road, in the area west of West Lake Avenue.

A gathering of men outside the Hollywood Photography Studio and the shoeshine parlor on Decatur Street.

Decatur Street

Story hour at the Auburn Branch Library.

People wait patiently in line to vote inside the E. R. Carter School.

REGISTERED VOTERS
MASS MEETING
Wheat St. Bapt. Church
Friday, May 10, 1946-8 p.m.
Miss Ella Baker,
N. A. A. C. P. Director of Branches
SPEAKER
Certificates Awarded All Block Workers

SPECIAL MUSIC

Don't Miss this great occasion.
Sponsored by All-Citizens Registration Committee

Mayor William Hartsfield is welcomed by Reverend Dorsey at the meeting of the National Baptist Alliance in 1945.

C. W. "Pete" Greenlea speaks at a mass rally at Wheat Street Baptist Church.

A view of Ashby Street, c. 1947.

Mary E. James, owner of the James Café on Hunter Street. The restaurant was one of the first African-American restaurants to receive an "A" rating from the city of Atlanta in 1946.

The City Auditorium is filled to capacity as African-Americans in Atlanta enjoy a concert by Ella Fitzgerald.

The construction of the Women's Dormitory at Morris Brown College was done by Aiken Construction Company, owned by "Chief" Walter Aiken, a longtime African-American contractor in Atlanta. Other buildings Aiken constructed include the Walluhaje in 1953. He also coached football and taught at Clark University (later Clark College) for many years.

The well-known Ralph Mays Troubadours performed at Atlanta night clubs and dances.

—MUSIC BY—

TROUBADOURS

Tomorrow Night, 9 till 1

Sunset Casino

Admission . . . Fee 31c 35 Cents
Tax 4c

The Silver Streak Grill was a popular eatery owned by Melvin Gaston. Years later the restaurant was sold to entrepreneur Henry Wynn, who opened Henry's Cabaret. Upstairs, the Blue Room featured live piano entertainment.

Club Zanzibar, a night spot on Auburn Avenue, was owned and operated by businessman Irwin Favors, his wife, Malinda, and son, Irwin, Jr. Though not as large as the Top Hat, it featured a full-course dinner, dancing, music by the Zanzibarons, and other local entertainers. The Favors also owned Champ's Pool Hall and a drycleaners. Year later, they would open the Auburn Avenue Casino.

Not all the socials and dances were held on Auburn Avenue. The Sunset Casino, later the Magnolia Ballroom, served as a popular venue for clubs, fraternities, and other organizations. Also on Atlanta's west side was the USO Club on Whitehouse Drive near the Washington High School, where the above group of partygoers are shown.

Three unidentified women on the "Avenue" in front of Hopkins Book Concern. Behind them is the neon marquee for the Poinciana Club, c. 1945. The Atlanta Daily World presently occupies the club's former spot.

This musical trio, the Triolets, performs for WEAS Radio, which allowed African-Americans to display their talents across the airwaves.

After losing his sight, photographer Harold S. Flanagan continued to operate his studio on Ashby Street with the aid of an assistant.

Jewel Woodward Simon is one of Atlanta's most prolific artists and sculptors. Her works were exhibited during the Negro Art Exhibitions at Atlanta University, organized by famed artist Hale Woodruff, whom she studied under. In 1967, she became the first African-American to graduate from the Atlanta College of Art.

This Boy Scout troop at Friendship Baptist Church (left) includes future mayor Maynard Holbrook Jackson, Jr. (2nd row, 3rd from left), whose father, Rev. Maynard H. Jackson, Sr. (right), succeeded Rev. E. R. Carter as pastor in 1945. He served until 1953.

Neighborhood baseball leagues and teams were very popular. This unidentified team has on several different uniforms, since city funds were very low for recreational activities for African-Americans.

Attorney Austin T. Walden, one of the founders of the Gate City Bar Association, represented an unidentified African-American during a court trial involving a racist hate group called the Columbians.

These young men attended the dedication of the Pittsburgh Branch of the YMCA.

Our Lady of Lourdes Mission, which operated the Catholic Colored People's Clinic in the 1940s and 1950s, used this vehicle to transport children. In the 1960s, it became Holy Family Hospital and is now known as Southwest Hospital and Medical Center.

Dr. Frederick Earl McLendon opened the McLendon Medical Clinic in 1946 on the corner of Sharon Street, off of Hunter Street.

The William A. Harris Memorial Hospital was located on Hunter Street.

Annual cultural performance of the "Colored" students of the Atlanta Public School system at the City Auditorium.

ic School Concert
April 25, 1

EDGAR ORR
ATLANTA

Andrew Jackson Lewis (left) was selected as the first principal of the John Hope Elementary School. Also pictured are Ira Jarrell, superintendent of the Atlanta Public Schools, and John Hope, Jr.

Herman J. Russell, a native Atlantan and resident of the Summerhill community, received the Roger Henderson Award in 1948 at David T. Howard High School, where he graduated.

The Atlanta Black Crackers, a member of the American League of the Negro League Baseball Teams, was organized in 1919. In 1937, John Harden, a service station owner, purchased the team to play at the Ponce de Leon Ballpark whenever the Atlanta Crackers (an all-white team) were not using the field. In 1938, the Black Crackers won the second half pennant of the American League. One of the bat boys for the Black Crackers was Othello "Chico" Renfroe, remembered as the "little kid" who used to tag along and ask the team a million questions. The Atlanta Black Crackers played to both African-American and mixed audiences. The era of the Atlanta Black Crackers ended in May 1949, when Harden announced that he would not field a team for that season.

Golfing for African-Americans in Atlanta had become a popular sport. Standing is Alfred "1up" Holmers at the Lincoln Country Club.

A contingency of Atlanta's African-American socialites at a reception for Roger and Ida Henderson.

In 1949, Langston Hughes (center) accepted an appointment as visiting professor at Atlanta University. During his stay he co-wrote a photo essay for Ebony *magazine on "Black" Atlanta, which appeared in a 1949 issue. He befriends photographer Griff Davis, a graduate of Morehouse who provided the photographs for the essay.*

Aerial view of the Morris Brown College campus, Hunter Street, and the Vine City community. The Joe Louis Gymnasium and the Herndon Stadium are both under construction. In the foreground to the left are the dormitories for Atlanta University.

The front entrance of the Alonzo Franklin Herndon Memorial Stadium, c. 1949.

Referees at Herndon Stadium, c. 1949.

The NAACP sponsored a program at the Greater Mount Calvary Baptist Church to honor the first eight African-American police officers in Atlanta, 1948. They are (l–r) Willie Elkins, Willard Strickland, John H. Sanders, Robert McKibbens, Ernest Lyons, Johnnie P. Jones, Henry Hooks, and Claude Dixon.

Car No. 333 transported some of the first African-American policemen, removing them from their walking beat. Shown are (l–r) Sgt. Claude Dixon and Sgt. Ernest Lyons.

Jesse B. Blayton purchased WERD Radio Station, becoming the first African-American in the country to own a radio station, 1949. Early disc jockeys included Jack "The Rapper" Gibson and James "Alley Pat" Patrick, who played a variety of music, including rhythm and blues, classical, and religious.

A view of Auburn Avenue looking west from the Herndon Building (top right). Note Bailey's Royal Theater marquee (right) and, farther up, the Royal Hotel signage. The Royal Hotel was owned and operated by Mrs. Carrie Cunningham, a well-known businesswoman and personality (top left). It was Mrs. Cunningham who bought and renovated the former Top Hat Club for her son, local musician Red McAllister, and changed the name to the Royal Peacock, because of her love for the exotic bird. Her sons's band performed nightly at the Royal Peacock, and the club attracted top-name entertainers (bottom). They resided at the Royal Hotel, whose lobby was filled with photographs of the numerous stars who stayed there. The club closed in the mid-1970s but has reopened periodically since then. The Royal Peacock continued to serve as a venue for local parties and dances, such as the party, pictured here, for Spelman graduates given by their parents in 1946.

Another venue for African-American parties, dances, and socials was the Skyroom on top of the City Auditorium. Shown enjoying the festivities are (l–r) William Brown, Nonye Strong Smith, Clarence Hubbard (a well-known local dancer), and Elizabeth Robinson, c. 1949.

The Atlanta Pictorial Reporter *was established in 1949 by photographer Herbert Hawkins. The paper concentrated on news of churches, schools, civic organizations, sports, and other social activities solely through pictures. It did not report any violent crimes or negative events. The publication's office was located in the Herndon Building on Auburn Avenue, c. 1949.*

Chapter 8

"And Justice for All,"
1950–1959

I am *somebody. . . .*

Rev. William Holmes Borders

1950 January 26. Ann Davis Lackey opens the South Chapel Grill on the corner of McDaniel and Chapel streets.

February. For the first time, five African-Americans are called for jury service in Atlanta.

Bishop Richard R. Wright, Jr., participates in the groundbreaking of the Phillis Wheatley YWCA new facility at Tatnall, Mitchell, and Hunter streets, which cost $147,000. (The building was completed a year later.)

Three miles of lighting from Decatur Street to Pryor, from Edgewood to Bell and Howell Street, and on Auburn Avenue from Ivy to Boulevard are dedicated at the Auburn Avenue Branch Carnegie Library. This dedication completes the opening of twenty-two miles of lighting by the Georgia Power Company in Atlanta.

A federal court sentences Fulton County officials to a year in jail and fines them for turning African-American prisoners over to a white mob, which beat them.

Over two hundred African-American parents and children file a petition against a segregated school system. It is denied.

The U.S. Supreme Court refuses to review a charge of discriminatory wage scales for Atlanta's African-American schoolteachers.

African-American golfer Howard Wheeler wins the 1950 Southern Open at the New Lincoln Country Club.

Eight hundred African-American children crowd the Royal Theater for a Christmas party sponsored by the YWCA and Davison's.

Dinah Washington, "Queen of the Blues," headlines a pre-Thanksgiving show at the City Auditorium.

Horace Ward is denied admission to the University of Georgia Law School.

1951 Roy Partridge opens Partridge Bakery on Hunter Street.

Dwelle Infirmary, located on Boulevard, is renamed Beaumont School of Practical Nursing. The school offers practical nursing courses to African-American women and a degree within six months. Tuition is $100 for the program or $5 a week.

"Chief" Walter Aiken builds the five-story Waluhaje Building on West Lake Avenue. It has a barber shop, jazz club, hotel, and apartments.

The Atlanta Branch of the NAACP hosts the 42nd Annual Conference. Officers present include Roy Wilkins and Thurgood Marshall.

Willie T. Menefee, owner of the popular Menefee's Restaurant, dies.

Ruby Blackburn organizes the Georgia League of Negro Women Voters.

Hopkins Book Concern closes.

A group of African-American students, along with A. J. Lewis, principal of John Hope Elementary School, travel to Washington, D.C., by train for the National Safety Patrol Convention.

Contaminated and poisonous whiskey is distributed to African-Americans in the Summerhill and other communities by John R. "Fat" Hardy, who is later arrested and convicted of murder. (Over 300 people became ill and 45 people died after consuming the whiskey. Hardy was sentenced to life in prison.)

The Tiger Flowers Taxi-Cab Service becomes the first metered service for African-Americans in Atlanta.

Dr. Hamilton Holmes, his sons Oliver and Tup, and businessman C. T. Bell file a lawsuit based on discrimination toward African-Americans playing on the public golf courses of the city of Atlanta.

The Paschal Brothers acquire property across the street from their restaurant on Hunter Street and construct Paschal's Restaurant.

Duke Ellington, Nat King Cole, and Sarah Vaughn perform at the City Auditorium. Admission is $2. The Booker T. Washington Mixed Choral Group performs during the intermission. An integrated group of 3,000 people attends.

1952
Eleven-year-old Ruby Mae Miles becomes the first patient admitted to the Hughes Spaulding Pavilion at Grady Hospital. The $2 million 125-bed facility admits 1,278 patients during its first year of operation. There are 26 African-American doctors. Dr. James B. Harris is president of the medical staff, and Grace T. Hamilton is secretary of the advisory board.

An agreement is presented by the Empire Real Estate Board, a group of African-American realtors, to help resolve the conflict over African-American expansion into Mozley Park.

There are 22,300 registered African-American voters in Atlanta.

October 14. The *Atlanta Daily World* endorses Dwight D. Eisenhower for president, and white newspapers in Atlanta endorse Adlai Stevenson.

Ernest Alexander establishes Aleck's Barbecue on Greensferry Avenue.

The Carver Public Housing Development is completed.

1953
June 30. Five African-American families are subjects of protest after moving into a neighborhood near Bankhead Highway. Police are called in.

Ernest Alexander

August. African-Americans in Atlanta roll out the red carpet for over thirty thousand Elks converging on the city for their national convention. The highlight of the convention is a colorful parade down Auburn Avenue featuring marching bands and Elk units. The Elks leave the city, according to a newspaper article about the event, knowing that out of 950 African-American-owned businesses, there are 119 beauty shops, 186 restaurants and sandwich shops, 89 grocery stores and markets, and 30 ice cream dealers.

October 5. African-Americans once again vote to reelect Mayor William Hartsfield.

November. Whitney Young is named director of the Atlanta University School of Social Work.

Life magazine features the production *Heaven Bound* in the article "Diabolical Doings in Atlanta."

The George Washington Carver Community Housing Project opens with 990 units. It is Atlanta's first postwar public housing project.

Dr. Rufus E. Clement, president of Atlanta University, is nominated in a citywide primary as the representative of the Third Ward to the Atlanta Board of Education.

Attorney A. T. Walden and Dr. Miles Amos are elected to the city Democratic Executive Committee. They are the first African-Americans since 1870 to hold a city office.

Cascade Heights community is annexed to the city of Atlanta. In the late 1960s and early 1970s, the racial composition of the community would change from white to African-American.

1954
April 5. The Atlanta Urban League criticizes the city for its slow pace in improving park facilities for African-Americans. They have access to only 158 acres of the 2,178 acres of park land. There are only two swimming pools for African-Americans and no public golf courses.

May. The Waluhaje Ballroom opens to the public, featuring dancer Grace Jackson, blues and ballad singer Zilla Mays, comic Baron Wilson from New York, and the Neal Montgomery Orchestra.

Albert E. Manley is elected as the first African-American and man to serve as president of Spelman College.

B. B. Beamon opens the Academy of Ballet Arts on West Hunter Street. Instruction includes ballet, tap, and interpretive dancing.

Walter White, Thurgood Marshall, and national officials and state presidents of the NAACP meet in Atlanta following the Supreme Court decision outlawing public school segregation.

Dr. George L. Hightower becomes the third Atlantan to be elected national president of Phi Beta Sigma. (The other two were R. A. Billings in 1945 and R. O. Johnson in 1949.)

Bronner Brothers purchase the former Silver Moon Bakery Shop for their beauty supply shop.

WAOK, Atlanta's second radio station for African-Americans, signs on the air.

1955

February. The National Press Club elects Louis Lautrer as president. An African-American reporter for the *Atlanta Daily World*, Lautrer is the first African-American to hold the position.

July–August. Horace Ward, a graduate of Morehouse College, attempts to enter the University of Georgia Law School.

July 13. The Atlanta Public Library affirms its position on desegregation, despite the U.S. Supreme Court decision.

August 1. African-American teachers are ordered to quit the NAACP or lose their teaching license. The order is later rescinded.

Atlanta native Walter White, executive secretary of the NAACP, dies. (He joined the NAACP in 1918 and served as an assistant to James Weldon Johnson.)

The first African-American deputies join the sheriff's department.

October 22. The first post office manned by African-Americans opens in Atlanta.

November 7. The U.S. Supreme Court declares segregation on Atlanta's golf courses unconstitutional. (The golf courses are integrated without incident.)

December 14. John Calhoun, president of the Atlanta Branch of the NAACP, is found guilty of contempt for refusing to turn over financial records to the Georgia State Revenue Commissioners. The branch is fined $25,000, and Calhoun becomes the first NAACP leader jailed since the Southern states began a crackdown on the association.

The Heman Perry Public Housing Development is completed on the northwest side of Atlanta.

Jacob and Freddye Henderson organize the first African-American travel agency in Atlanta.

Charles Lincoln Harper dies.

Citizens Trust Bank opens its West Side Office on Hunter Street.

1956

There are 24,888 registered African-American voters in Atlanta.

Forbes magazine names Auburn Avenue as the "Richest Negro Street in the World."

The Atlanta Public Teachers Association votes to withdraw from the American Federation of Teachers (AFL-CIO) rather than admit African-American members.

The Auburn Avenue Casino has its grand opening of the Rainbow Room, featuring Lavern

Baker singing "Tweedle Dee." Admission is $1.75 in advance, $2.00 at the door.

Mount Zion Baptist Church moves into its new sanctuary on Boulevard. Atlanta's African-American cinematographer, J. E. Jordan, films the event.

Gospel promoter Herman Nash presents in concert the Soul Stirrers, featuring Sam Cooke, Rev. C. L. Franklin, and the Ward Singers, at the City Auditorium.

Judge Charles Wofford installs the officers of the League of Negro Women Voters. Ruby Blackburn is president and Whitney Young gives the challenge.

Nat King Cole, fearful of violence over the racial segregation issue, cancels a scheduled appearance at the City Auditorium. (An estimated 2,000 persons—mostly white plus about 500 African-American patrons—had purchased tickets. Cole's Atlanta scheduled appearance came a week after he was assaulted on the stage of the Birmingham Municipal Auditorium. Other leading African-American entertainers, including Lena Horne, Sammy Davis, Jr., and Dorothy Dandridge refused to make personal appearances in Atlanta because of fear of racial incidents.)

Native Atlantan Mattiwilda Dobbs makes her first hometown appearance since becoming a member of the Metropolitan Opera Company. Her performance is at Wheat Street Baptist Church.

1957

January 9. Rev. William Holmes Borders and other African-American ministers attempt to integrate buses.

January 10–11. The Southern Negro Leaders Conference on Transportation and Nonviolent Integration is organized by sixty African-Americans from ten Southern states who meet in Atlanta to discuss organizational strategies for integration in the South. The organization's name is later changed to the Southern Christian Leadership Conference.

January. The Atlanta Branch of the NAACP sponsors the first Freedom Dinner.

January. Professor Howard Zinn and several young women from Spelman College attempt to sit in the "whites-only" section of the gallery of the Georgia Assembly.

September. Consolidated Mortgage and Investment Company is formed to assist African-Americans in obtaining real estate loans; collecting mortgages; buying, selling, owning, and leasing property; and making investments. A. T. Walden is elected president; W. L. Calloway, executive vice-president; T. M. Alexander, treasurer.

WERD Radio Station signs off the air. It is sold and relocated.

The Joel Chandler Harris Homes are built. (The 510 units were to serve as a white buffer on the encroachment of African-American neighborhoods.)

Theodore M. Alexander runs for alderman.

Billie "Lady Day" Holiday performs at the Magnolia Ballroom.

L. J. Fuller opens the Fuller Realty Company on the corner of Chestnut and Hunter streets.

Joseph Bickers opens a realty company that would be one of the few successful businesses started in Auburn during this period.

1958

January 11. Ten parents and their children file suit in federal court declaring an end to segregation in the Atlanta Public School System.

April 7. The Atlanta Branch of the NAACP charges that African-American communities such as Vine City and Buttermilk Bottom are being left out of the city's urban renewal program.

November 14. Mayor William Hartsfield urges the General Assembly to allow Atlantans to decide whether to close schools or keep them open despite integration. (An integrated school under state law could not receive public funding and would thus automatically be closed.)

Asa T. Yancey is named medical director of the Hugh Spaulding Pavilion of Grady

Memorial Hospital.

Singer Chuck Willis, a native of Atlanta, known as the "King of the Stroll" and "The Sheik of the Shake," is killed in a car wreck.

University Barbershop opens on the corner of Chestnut and Hunter streets.

January 9. Atlanta's segregated bus system is declared unconstitutional by a federal court. (African-American ministers urged their congregations not to test the decision immediately.)

May 19. Mrs. Maynard Jackson integrates the Atlanta Public Library by receiving a library card.

June 5. School desegregation is declared illegal in Atlanta by a court ruling.

Attorney Leroy Johnson is admitted to the Georgia Bar Association.

Columbus Calvin "Duke" Pearson, Jr., a native of the Summerhill community, a graduate of David T. Howard High School, and a former member of the Clark College band, arrives in New York and works at the Count Basie Bar. (He eventually worked for Donald Byrd, the Benny Goodson Jazztet, and Dakota Staton and became the personal accompanist for Nancy Wilson.)

Promoter B. B. Beamon presents a check to Warren R. Cochran, director of the YMCA, for ten boys to attend boarding camp at Lake Allatoona.

Lots are offered for sale for the Carroll Heights and Fairlane Heights subdivisions in the Adamsville section of town. The communities are developed off of Bolton Road.

Miss E. A. Ware (center) and her court pose next to the car that carried them in a parade. The E. A. Ware Elementary School was located on Hunter Street.

Members of the Southern Intercollegiate Athletic Conference relax after a dinner meeting. The SIAC was organized to facilitate and govern athletic programs at African-American colleges in the South.

Morris Brown College students await their turn to donate blood to the Red Cross during a blood drive held in the Joe Louis Gymnasium, 1950.

The Atlanta Branch of the NAACP, under the leadership of Charles L. Harper, hosted the forty-second annual convention in 1951. The delegates are posing in front of the Municipal Auditorium.

To The People Of Atlanta:

Poison moonshine is being shipped into Atlanta. Your doctor will tell you that it is dangerous to drink.

State and Federal authorities say that this moonshine has caused blindness and even death.

Any person offering you a drink of moonshine certainly is not a friend, but a person who is violating the law and who has no regard for your health.

Be Smart-Play Safe
Don't Drink
MOONSHINE.

Contaminated and poisonous whiskey was distributed to African-Americans in the Summerhill community and other areas by John R. (Tuts) Hardy, who was later arrested and convicted of murder. Over 300 people became ill and 45 people died after consuming the whiskey. Hardy was sentenced to life in prison.

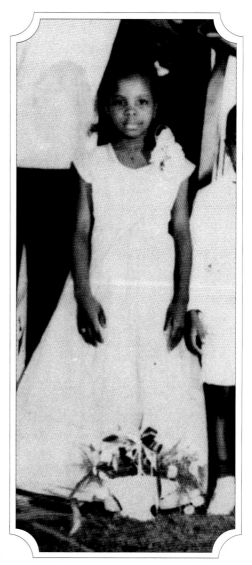

Before Gladys Maria Knight went off to New York to win the Ted Mack Amateur Hour in 1952, she was selected as "Little Miss Morris Brown College," c. 1950.

The Butler Street Grocery Store and Grill, facing south toward downtown and Edgewood Avenue.

A variety of housing could be located in one block. Here, at Auburn Avenue and Butler Street, were a two-story apartment building and two-story duplexes. Between them is one of hundreds of churches in the heart of the African-American community.

Looking east at the corner of Ashby and Gordon streets (now Ralph D. Abernathy Drive), 1952. To the right is St. Anthony's Catholic Church, which today has a predominately African-American congregation. In the foreground is Sears, Roebuck & Co., where in the 1960s one of the first African-American Santa Clauses appeared in Atlanta.

Residents of the Carrie Steele Pitts Orphanage surround one of the dorm mothers. The orphans home was founded in 1892 by Carrie Steele Logan, a former slave. It's first location was on Auburn Avenue.

The intersection of Fairburn and Campbellton roads, looking west. In 1954, when this picture was taken, the area was called Ben Hill, Georgia. The Texaco station and C. R. Suber's Feedstore have been replaced by a convenience store and service station. African-Americans began moving to this area in the late 1960s and early 1970s.

This view looks west down Gordon Road crossing Peyton Road. It was also the route to Adamsville, Georgia, later to be annexed to the city of Atlanta.

Flanagan Service Station, at the corner of Auburn Avenue and Bell Street, was later converted into a dry cleaners. Currently, the city of Atlanta has a police precinct on the spot. In the background is a side view of the Herndon Building, the second largest building for African-American professionals in Atlanta. It also housed the Savoy Hotel and Ballroom and Kelly's Photography Studio, c. 1950.

WERD disc jockeys

James "Alley Pat" Patrick

Attorney Austin T. Walden and Dr. Miles Amos, owner of Amos Drug Store, signed a document as they became the first African-Americans elected to the Atlanta Democratic Executive Committee, 1953. They were the first African-Americans since 1870 to be elected to office in Atlanta.

PLEASE VOTE FOR AN EDUCATOR
ABLE · HONEST · CONSCIENTIOUS

DR. RUFUS E. CLEMENT
(PRESIDENT OF ATLANTA UNIVERSITY)

**for membership on
Board of Education**

CANDIDATE FROM THIRD WARD
YOUR VOTE WILL BE
GREATLY APPRECIATED
CITY WIDE PRIMARY ELECTION
MAY 13, 1953

The Prince Hall Masonic Building was constructed on the corner of Auburn Avenue and Hilliard Street in 1946. In 1955, an elevator was installed and additions made to accommodate the expanding lodges. The first Masonic Lodge organized among African-Americans in Atlanta was the Saint James Lodge No. 4 F. & A.M. in 1871, with Rev. Francis J. Peck, pastor of Big Bethel A.M.E. Church, as the worshipful master.

A view down McDaniel Street, in the Pittsburgh community. The Harlem Theater, in the heart of the community, featured live shows and movies, c. 1953.

O. T. Bell cleared the block at Auburn and Piedmont and constructed the first modernized motel on Auburn Avenue, known as the Bellview Motel, later renamed the Palamount Motel.

The University Hotel located on Davis Street (now Northside Drive) offered visitors to the city the latest modern conveniences in hospitality and lodging. Located near the Atlanta University schools, the hotel featured a small jazz club. The building, along with an African-American community known as "Lightning," was demolished in 1990 for construction of the Georgia Dome.

Whitney Young, future executive director of the National Urban League and dean of the School of Social Work at Atlanta University, speaks to a group at the Hawks Dinette, a popular restaurant located on Auburn Avenue.

During the traditional homecoming activities at the Atlanta University schools, each fraternity selected a queen. The Phi Beta Sigma fraternity at Morris Brown College chose Deloris Harris, a native of Jacksonville, Florida, as its Miss Sigma for 1954.

It was an annual tradition for the seventh-grade class of the Thomas Heathe Slater Elementary School in south Atlanta to pose for a group photo on the day of the promotional exercises.

The Thomas Heathe Slater school opened in the early 1950s in south Atlanta and served the Carver Homes and High Point communities.

After Clark College moved from south Atlanta to the west side, where Atlanta University Center was located, new dormitories were needed to accommodate the increasing student population. Kresgie Hall was completed around 1955.

The Sigma Gamma Rho sorority began the tradition of sponsoring the debutante ball for young African-American women in Atlanta. The balls were held at the City Auditorium until it was demolished in 1980. They are now held every December at the Atlanta Civic Center.

The 1954 presentation of "The Wedding of Roses" at Big Bethel A.M.E. Church. The traditional pageant was established in 1944.

On January 9, 1957, at 10:30 A.M., the Triple L Movement (Love, Liberty, Loyalty) went into effect as local ministers, including William Holmes Borders, Rev. Martin Luther King, Sr., and Rev. Samuel Williams, were hauled off to jail in a paddy wagon. The charges were that they had violated Georgia segregation laws. For their ride of about thirty-six blocks, they had occupied front seats in a public bus that were normally reserved for white passengers. The driver of the bus asked them to leave through the rear door, but they exited through the front door. They were jailed temporarily until they posted $1,000 bond each.

Two stalwarts in the African-American community, Rev. Emory Searcy and grandmaster John Wesley Dobbs, assist in hanging the cornerstone for the Mount Zion Second Baptist Church located on the corner of Boulevard and Irwin Street, c. 1956.

Even though the Supreme Court outlawed segregation on all public buses, riders still remained segregated. State officials said that Georgia was not a party to the South Carolina legal action and would not be immediately affected, c. 1956.

Adjusting his academic hood is Representative Adam Clayton Powell, outspoken congress-
man from Harlem, New York, who gave a commencement address at Morehouse College.
He is proceeded by trustee Trevor Arnett and followed by Dr. Benjamin Elijah Mays,
president of Morehouse College, 1956.

School teacher Helena Rivers and her orderly line of students await a schoolbus after a performance at the City Auditorium. Segregated perfor-
mances were held for African-American children in the Atlanta Public School System.

Looking west down Hunter Street.

Jesse B. Blayton's Night School Division holds its graduation dance at the Royal Peacock Club.

These children appear happy, despite their living conditions. In many areas in Atlanta where federal public housing did not replace all of the slum housing, thousands of African-American families lived in filth and squalor. Here, a wall was used for solving math problems and games of tick-tack-toe. The man and children are unidentified, c. 1953.

Ruby Blackburn demonstrates a voting machine at the A. F. Herndon Elementary School, c. 1959.

Ruby Blackburn was one of the most prolific civic-minded leaders of the African-American community. She founded and established numerous community organizations, as the campaign flyer attests.

The National Convention of Links met at Atlanta University during the summer of 1957.

LEAGUE OF NEGRO WOMEN VOTERS INC.

"EDUCATION IN POLITICS"

219½ AUBURN AVE., N. E.

Heavyweight boxing champion Joe Louis, a frequent visitor to Atlanta, is greeted by Marion Jackson (center), sports editor of the Atlanta Daily World, *at the 100% Wrong Club annual banquet.*

Atlanta's white community had the Varsity, and the African-American community had the Split T Drive-In Restaurant, located at the corner of Mayson-Turner Avenue and Simpson Street.

Crossing Auburn Avenue at the corner of Piedmont, 1959.

Surrounded by an entourage is local entertainer Billy Wright, the man from whom, according to oral legend, Little Richard borrowed the idea of wearing the pompadour hairstyle and pancake makeup. Wright performed at the Poinciana Club, the Royal Peacock Club, and numerous other venues in Atlanta. He died in 1991.

B. B. Beamon (left) not only established himself as a promoter of acts and entertainment but also supported charitable causes. Here he is shown with the great Nat King Cole (center) and local promoter Herman Nash (right), who provided Atlanta with the best gospel talent during the 1950s and 1960s.

Singer Jackie Wilson, sprawled out on the Magnolia Ballroom stage, was no stranger to Atlanta nightclubs and venues. A former boxer from Detroit, Wilson was promoted by Supersonic Attractions, the mega booking and promotions company owned by well-known Atlantan Henry Wynn. Wynn, shown here with photojournalist Harmon Perry (left) and unidentified man, owned Henry's Grill, Henry's Cabaret, the New Royal Peacock Club, the Red Top Cab Company, and the Morocco Club. He was one of Atlanta's most enterprising African-Americans.

One of the tallest structures in the Summerhill community was the Allen Temple A.M.E. Church. The edifice was razed to make way for the Atlanta Stadium, and a new church was built on the corner of West Lake Avenue and Simpson Road in the 1960s.

A fine example of powerful gothic architecture, Wheat Street Baptist Church served as a prominent meeting place, hosting mass rallies, civil rights meetings, plays, and pageants. The church has been pastored by outstanding men, including Rev. Peter James Bryant, Rev. Henderson, and Rev. William Holmes Borders, who coined the phrase "I Am Somebody" long before Rev. Jesse Jackson made it a popular saying.

Berean Academy kindergarten graduation class, 1958.

Alexander L. Adams operated a photo studio on West Lake Avenue. He was very sought after by groups and organizations in the African-American community in the 1950s and 1960s.

Horace Ward (left) a lawyer who attempted to enter the University of Georgia Law School, is shown with Constance Motley, attorney for the NAACP, and attorney Donald L. Hollowell, who represented Ward in his suit against the University of Georgia.

WERD broadcasts a press conference featuring Jackie Robinson.

Wheat Street Baptist Church nursery pageant

Charles W. Lowe, a former tailor, captured the images of families and social and civic events. He operated his studio from his home.

The Bonner-Pearsons

The Conleys

The Dobbs

The Kings

The Scotts

Chapter 9

"I Have a Dream," 1960–1969

***M**aybe the need in America is not white power or black power, but "striped power," where black and white work together.*

Martin Luther King, Jr.

1960

September 11. The Honorable Elijah Muhammad, messenger of Allah, speaks at the Sunset Casino.

December 23. La Carrousel, a night club and lounge, opens at Paschal's Hotel.

There are 34,642 registered voters in the African-American community in Atlanta.

Twenty-two Atlanta University students are arrested and sentenced to ten days for sit-in demonstrations. A few days later Mayor William Hartsfield orders their release from jail.

Seventy-seven students are arrested at sit-in demonstrations at ten restaurants in downtown Atlanta. They are charged with sit-in conspiracy. They invite presidential candidates Richard Nixon and John F. Kennedy to Atlanta.

Martin Luther King, Jr., and his family return to Atlanta. King becomes co-pastor of Ebenezer Baptist Church with his father.

Rhythm Rink, the only roller skating facility for African Americans in Atlanta, opens on Simpson Road.

1961

March. The city of Atlanta hires its first African-American truck driver.

March. African-American dentists are expelled from the Thomas P. Hinman Clinic at the City Auditorium.

May 6. Dr. Harry V. Richardson is inaugurated as the first president of the Interdenominational Theological Center. The center consists of Gammon Theological Seminary (Methodist, 1883), Morehouse School of Religion (Baptist, 1884), Phillips School of Theology (C.M.E., 1944), and Turner School of Religion (A.M.E., 1900).

May 13. The Freedom Riders are due in Atlanta from Washington, D.C.

May. Patrolman A. A. Harris becomes the first African-American policeman assigned to traffic duty. He is assigned to the intersection of Ashby and Hunter streets.

June. Atlanta gets its first African-American bus drivers.

August. The first African-American Negro housing inspector is hired.

Georgia Tech accepts its first African-American students.

The Simpson Road–Dixie Hills community is rapidly developing a number of African-American businesses. The Hightower Road, West Lake, and Verbena Street areas are included. Such businesses are the Sam Carrol Tea Shack, the Flamingo Grill, Parker's Drug Store, the Simpson Road West Lake Shopping Center (which houses the Music Inn), Jordan's Beauty and Barber Shop, Cooper's Self Service Drugs, and Simpson Dinette. There are five African-American-owned service stations.

Major shops and restaurants in the downtown central business district are desegregated following an agreement between white and black leaders.

Development begins on the Collier Heights community, located in northwest Atlanta between Collier Road and Bankhead Highway. African-Americans begin purchasing homes, and it becomes one of the most exclusive communities for African-Americans in Atlanta.

The Committee on Appeal for Human Rights publishes a full-page ad in the local newspapers. The document, called "A Time to Speak," deals with recent store boycotts and the committee's pledge not to endorse or support political candidates but to continue to fight for human rights.

Sam Cooke headlines a spring concert at the City Auditorium with B. B. King, Etta James, Chuck Berry, the Drifters, and Joe Tex. Admission is $2.

Atlantan Gladys Knight makes her first appearance at the Apollo Theater.

John Wesley Dobbs dies. Though he attended the First Congregational Church on Courtland, he asked to be funeralized on Auburn Avenue. His services takes place at Big Bethel A.M.E. Church.

Turner High School graduates Hamilton Holmes and Charlayne Hunter integrate the University of Georgia.

Nine African-American students integrate four white high schools: Grady, Northside, Brown, and Murphy high schools.

Ivan Allen is elected mayor by the combined votes of African-Americans and the middle- to upper-class whites. He defeats Lester Maddox.

Dorothy Alexander opens an interior decorating business.

The Dixie Hill Apartments and Shopping Center, featuring a variety of shops and stores, opens at Verbena Street and Shirley Place.

Ralph A. Long, Lawrence Williams, and Ford Greene are accepted into Georgia Tech. Ten other African-Americans are rejected.

The Fun Bowl, the first ten-pin bowling lane for African-Americans in Atlanta, opens on Mason Turner Road.

B. B. Beamon and his partner Herman Nash buy the Savoy Hotel, located in the Herndon Building on Auburn Avenue. Beamon opens a 24-hour restaurant next to the hotel.

The city of Atlanta hires its first African-American firemen.

1962

October 1. Dogwood Lanes, a 24-lane bowling alley, is opened on Bankhead Highway.

December 18. The "Peyton Wall" is erected at Peyton and Harlan roads in southwest Atlanta to deter African-Americans from buying and moving into the Cascade Heights neighborhood. The action is approved by the Board of Aldermen upon the recommendation of Mayor Ivan Allen.

Ralph Long, Jr., and Albert Brooks become the first African-American men to participate in the City Tennis Tournament at the Bitsy Grant Tennis Center.

NAACP delegates attending the Fifty-third Annual Convention picket downtown establishments, including the ribs and barbecue restaurant operated by Lester Maddox, for their refusal to accommodate delegates.

Mr. and Mrs. T. M. Alexander, Margaret Davis Bowen, and others integrate the opening performance of the Metropolitan Opera at the Fox Theater.

The Thomasville Residential Housing development, opens.

Grady Hospital is seized by African-American students protesting the segregation of the hospital. Twenty-three are arrested.

Nash's General Auto Repairs opens on Simpson Street across from the Rainbow Inn.

The first African-American intern begins work at Grady Hospital.

Atlanta musician Cleveland Lyons, well-known leader of the Cleveland Lyons Combo who backed the Pips and Little Clarence, dies.

Georgia State University is integrated.

Ruby Doris Smith, a student at Spelman College, is jailed in Jackson, Mississippi, for sixty days for her participation as a Freedom Rider.

Sidney Poitier appears in a press conference in southwest Atlanta and says that he will not waste his talent in the "one-dimensional" television field.

Grady Hospital appoints Dr. Asa Yancey as the first African-American "resident staff member."

Herman J. Russell, owner of H. J. Russell Plastering Company, becomes the first African-American member of the Atlanta Chamber of Commerce.

Theodore M. Alexander, Rod Harris, and Leroy Johnson enter the Georgia state senate race.

Attorney Leroy R. Johnson is elected the first African-American senator since 1870.

1963   January. The Fulton County Superior Court orders the "Peyton Wall" down after the Board of Aldermen and Mayor Allen refuse to have the barrier removed.

African-American students integrate Emory University.

African-American demonstrators hold a "lie-in" at Grady Hotel to protest segregation of the city's hotels.

Theaters are integrated.

African-American representatives of nine organizations recommend a local public accommodations act, an open-occupancy housing law, establishment of "fair employment," desegregation of public schools and facilities, and the appointment of African-Americans to judgeships.

Dr. Martin Luther King, Jr., makes a public appearance in a rally at Hurt Park at the request of the African-American community. The rally is sponsored by the Summit Leadership Conference.

Atlanta mayor Ivan Allen proclaims May 6–13 as United Negro College Fund Week in Atlanta.

Wheat Street Baptist Church becomes one of the first African-American churches to sponsor a housing program when Wheat Street Gardens is completed.

Dr. Martin Luther King, Jr., wins the Nobel Peace Prize.

1964   February. Attorney Austin T. Walden is sworn into office by Mayor Ivan Allen as a "stand by" judge for the municipal and traffic court of Atlanta.

Acres of the Summerhill community are razed to make way for the construction of the new Atlanta Stadium.

The Bowen Housing Project, named for Bishop J. W. E. Bowen, opens.

Judge A. T. Walden

SNCC (Student Nonviolent Coordinating Committee) launches a campaign against segregated restaurants. The NAACP campaigns against segregated hotels. The Southern Christian Leadership Conference and the All-Citizens Committee launch a voter-education campaign.

African-Americans picket the Bailey Theater chain in an effort to convince the manager to upgrade salaries of African-American employees and promote cleanliness.

Andrew Young is named executive director of the Southern Christian Leadership Conference. (In 1967, he became executive vice-president.)

1965   September 19. Q. V. Williamson is elected as the first African-American alderman in Atlanta since 1870.

Faye Burress, owner of numerous beauty salons for African American women in Atlanta, is appointed by Governor Carl Sanders to the Georgia State Board of Cosmetology, becoming the first African-American on the board.

The Majority to Minority plan (M to M) is implemented, allowing students to transfer from a school in which they are in the majority to a school in which they are in the minority.

The Catholic Colored People's Clinic is accredited and renamed the Holy Family Hospital.

Grace Towns Hamilton is elected as the first African-American woman in the Georgia legislature.

President Lyndon B. Johnson signs the historic Civil Rights Act of 1964, which opens the doors of restaurants, hotels, and theaters to African-Americans in Atlanta and elsewhere.

Dr. Martin Luther King, Jr., is honored with a biracial dinner at the Biltmore Hotel following his receipt of the 1964 Nobel Peace Prize.

Grady Hospital begins to admit African-Americans.

The Paladium (formerly the Dogwood Bowling Lanes) on Bankhead Highway has its grand opening with Brook Benton, Lavern Baker, and Cannonball Adderly.

Nina Simone headlines a big jazz show at the Magnolia Ballroom.

Colonel Austin T. Walden dies. His funeral is featured in *Jet* magazine.

Construction magnate and former football coach "Chief" Walter H. Aiken, dies. His company constructed a large percentage of the African-American community between the 1920s and 1950s, including the Waluhaje Apartment Hotel, the West Lake Court Apartments, a section of houses in the Fair Street–Rosser Street areas, and the Women's Dormitory of Morris Brown College.

Dr. Hamilton M. Holmes, Sr., dies.

The World Heavyweight Championship fight between Cassius Clay and Floyd Patterson is shown on closed-circuit screens at the Paul Jones Sports Arena on Memorial Drive and Chester Avenue. Tickets range between $4 and $6.

Flipper Temple A.M.E. Church burns its mortgage. Rev. Julius Williams is pastor.

Kansas state senator George Haley, brother of author Alex Haley, tours Atlanta with Georgia state senators Leroy Johnson and Horace Ward. All three graduated in the same class from Morehouse College.

Vice-president Hubert H. Humphrey speaks before the David T. Howard High School student body.

The new Carrie Steele Pitts Orphanage is dedicated on Fairburn Road. Mae Yates is director.

1966

January 10. Representative Julian Bond is refused a seat in the Georgia House of Representatives for speaking out against the Vietnam War.

Led by Stokely Carmichael, the chairman of SNCC who denounces the latest instance of police brutality, the Summerhill Riot takes place, and one person is killed. The riot is triggered by the shooting of an African-American male, an alleged auto thief, by an Atlanta policeman. Mayor Ivan Allen summons twenty-five of the city's leading African-American ministers, including Rev. Samuel Williams, to attempt to restore peace and order.

Civil rights demonstrators led by Dr. King rush officers of the Georgia State Patrol in an attempt to enter the state capitol during a demonstration protesting the Georgia House's barring of Representative-elect Julian Bond. Bond, a twenty-six-year-old civil rights worker, is refused his seat because of statements denouncing U.S. participation in Vietnam and his opposition of the draft.

The sole African-American shoeshine boy at the state capitol loses customers as a new electric shoeshine machine is installed.

1967   June 19–20. Stokely Carmichael and four other African-American men are arrested, and racial unrest occurs where one man is killed and three others are wounded.

Hosea Williams and a group of African-American citizens confront the Atlanta Board of Education demanding an end to double sessions in three high schools. They also demand that more African-Americans be appointed to administrative jobs in the school system.

Xernona Clayton

1968   Xernona Clayton becomes the first African-American to host a prime-time television program. (Her program "Themes and Variations," later changed to the "Xernona Clayton Show," ran from 1968 to 1975.)

Hundreds of thousands of people converge upon the city to mourn the death of Dr. Martin Luther King, Jr., who was assassinated in Memphis, Tennessee. The funeral at Ebenezer Baptist Church is televised nationally.

Maynard Holbrook Jackson, grandson of John Wesley Dobbs, is defeated in the U.S. Senate race against Herman Talmadge, even though Jackson carries the Atlanta vote.

Harmon Perry, veteran photographer for the *Atlanta Daily World*, becomes the first African-American reporter for the *Atlanta Journal*, two years after he made his first attempt to seek employment there. His first story is the assassination of Dr. Martin Luther King, Jr.

Katherine Jefferson assumes ownership of House of Murphy Printing Company.

State Representative Julian Bond is presented to the 1968 Democratic National Convention as a vice-presidential candidate.

1969   Dr. Horace E. Tate, veteran educator and first-term member of the Atlanta School Board, announces his candidacy for mayor of Atlanta, becoming the first African-American to make such a declaration in the 120-year history of the city. Tate draws 23 percent of the vote in the primary. Vice-Mayor Sam Massell wins the election.

Maynard H. Jackson becomes vice-mayor under Sam Massell, and the number of African-American aldermen increases from one to five.

Dr. Benjamin E. Mays is elected to the Atlanta Board of Education.

Amos Drug Store closes after forty-six years of service.

Dr. Martin Luther King, Jr., makes his first public speech in Atlanta during the civil rights movement at a rally in Hurt Park, 1960.

THE ATLANTA INQUIRER

The power of the
Pen is mightier
than the Sword.

"To seek out the truth and report
it impartially without Fear or Favor"

PUBLISHED WEEKLY BY
Ware Printing and Publishing Co.
Post Office Box 9215, Station B
ATLANTA 14, GEORGIA

VOL. ONE   TEL. PL. 8-7478   SUNDAY, JULY 31, 1960   TEN CENTS   No. 1

Looking . . . . Forward
BY bill strong

A NEWSPAPER IS BORN

"This We Pledge"

TIME TO TAKE A STAND

There is a time for all things. A time for thought, a time for speculation, a time for investigation, but most assuredly this is not a time for straddling the fence.

The American Negro (especially in the South) is engaged in a gigantic life or death struggle with the foes of human decency. The twin evils of segregation and discrimination have been dealt mortal blows. Yet their disciples, the gradualists, the reactionaries, the hate peddlers are waging a last ditch stand in an effort to keep them alive. But there is only one hope for their salvation, "to turn back the clock." This cannot be done. History moves forward, not backward, and any efforts, however mighty, to thwart operation of this natural phenomenon can lead only to stagnation and eventual destruction. The pages of history are covered with accounts of once powerful empires, whose leaders undertook to halt the march of time. Theirs is a grim lesson for the world.

Yet, here in a time when the Negro is in need of a forth-right, vigorous, courageous leadership, what do we find in our own ranks. We find those, whose positions cover them with the indicia of leadership, giving lip service to our cause, while publicly decrying our methods, urging gradualism and restraint (go slow), sowing seeds of dissension among our ranks — straddling the fence, "shades of Uncle Tom."

Is it possible that some of us occupying positions of leadership are trying to stay the hand of fate? Do we recognize that the old order is in its death throes and with its passing, our influence also passes? If the answer to these questions is yes, I say to you, step down, retire gracefully from the scene, pass on the mantle of leadership to a younger, more able personality — No man can stop the march of history, fight it and be destroyed.

This is a time for taking a stand. Gradualism died in Greensboro, N. C., February 1,

Voters League Presents Candidates

Registered voters will have an opportunity to hear the nine contesting candidates in the September 14 Primary Election at the Annual Meeting of the Atlanta Negro Voters League, in Big Bethel AME Church, Thursday, August 4, at 8:00 P.M. The annual election of officers, members of the standing committees as well as ward and precinct leaders nominated in their respective sections, will be held at the same meeting.

A. T. Walden and Rev. Wm. M. Jackson, co-chairmen of the League, are urging that every registered voter in Fulton County attend this important meeting. Those persons elected will serve as members of the executive committee of the organization until the next Annual Election.

1960, the day the first student sat down at a white lunch counter and asked for service. Since that time wakes have been held for it all over the South — at some there was rejoicing, at others mourning. There is only one course of action open to our leadership. You must either join hands and lead us together down the path of freedom or step aside.

I need not discuss here the dangers of "fence straddling." It suffices to say, the present need is for positive dynamic leadership. The Negro community cannot afford the luxury of public pronunciations, from its so called leaders, advocating a doctrine of stop, wait and see — do nothing. Such ill advised statements have the effect of giving aid and comfort to our enemies, the foes of human decency. This is a new day, the dawn of a new era, let us close ranks and demand, as one, our rights as free men in a free society.

WANTED
Newsboys
Call
PL 8-7478

SCLC HOLDS WORKSHOP

ATLANTA, GEORGIA — A two-day community workshop on the philosophy and techniques of non-violent resistance will be held at the Butler Street YMCA on Thursday and Fri-

DR. M. L. KING, JR.

day, August 4th and 5th.

The workship is opened to the public and is designed to provide opportunity for students, ministers and community leaders to delve deeper into the principles and practices of this relatively new instrument for social change, and to evaluate its practical implications for the Atlanta area. The opening session is scheduled for ten o'clock Thursday morning, August 4th; and the program will continue with afternoon and evening sessions on Thursday, and morning and afternoon sessions on Friday, August 5th.

Dr. Martin L. King, Jr., president of the Southern Christian Leadership Conference and internationally known advocate of the non-violent movement in America, will be a principal speaker and discussion leader. Other workshop leaders announced by the Southern Christian Leadership Conference are the Reverend Wyatt Tee Walker, who will assume the executive directorship of SCLC on August 1; and the Reverend Samuel W. Williams, president of the Atlanta Branch NAACP, and pastor of the Friendship Baptist Church. Rev. Williams, who is also a vice-president of

(Continued on Page 2)

Today marks the birth of a new publication in the City of Atlanta. It is the brain child of a group of young men, who felt that a void existed in the reporting of news in the "Atlanta Negro Community." It is their desire to fill this void by publishing a newspaper dedicated to the advancement of those principles which best serve the interests of the "Atlanta Negro Community" as a whole. They have pledged themselves to a fair and impartial reporting of the news and to take a firm unequivocal stand on controversial issues involving the interests of our group.

The Atlanta Inquirer shall endeavor at all times to reflect sincerity, honesty and integrity and be a credit to the City of Atlanta. Your support, cooperation and criticism is earnetly solicited.

STUDENT COMMITTEE LAUDS BLAIR

The Student Non-violent Coordinating Committee, representative spokesman for the student protest movement against discrimination, has wired Greensboro student, Mr. Ezell Blair, Jr., congratulations for the fact that, on July 25, 1960, Woolworth and Kress of Greensboro integrated their lunch counters. Mr. Blair, a freshman at A & T College in Greensboro, was among the four Negro students who, on February 1, 1960, staged the first lunch counter sit-in and thus heralded the beginning of the nation-wide student non-violent movement.

In letters of congratulation to Mr. Blair and other student leaders, the Student Non-violent Coordinating Committee has expressed the feeling that "July 25th, bringing the integration of the Greensboro lunch counters, is a profoundly significant date in the movement of one cycle". The significance stems from the fact, according to the Coordinating Committee, that "these same stores, only five months ago refused service to Negroes and, in so doing, became the symbol of injustice and second-class citizenship". This refusal "set off a chain of non-violent direct action by Negro students long dissatisfied with their enforced second-class status and by white students who had long felt the contradictions in the American way of life".

Jane Stembridge, secretary of the Coordinating Committee, stated that "what happened in Greensboro, the kick-off place, can happen and is happening all across the South. People can come to an understanding, barriers can be removed, a new South can be born, and

Reader's Note

Beginning with the next edition of this publication, a section will be devoted to printing the letters of citizens, in the community, who desire to make a public expression on certain issues. All readers are encouraged to submit to us any comments they desire printed. As nearly as space permits, being governed by good taste and journalistic practice, all letters received will be printed. All letters should be typewritten, doublespaced, and limited to not more than 100 words in length. They should be addressed to Editor, Atlanta Inquirer, P. O. Box 9215, Atlanta, Georgia. Any letters received which are unsigned and without complete return address will not be printed.

America can become an actual democracy".

The secretary also reported that Mr. Marion S. Barry, Jr., Nashville student and chairman of the Student Non-violent Coordinating Committee, and Mr. Bernard Lee, expelled student from Alabama State, who represented the student committee before both the Democratic and Republican Platform Committees, will give their reports to the student coordinating body at its August 5th-7th meeting to be held at Morehouse Col-

(Continued on Page 2)

The first copy of the Atlanta Inquirer, *July 31, 1960.*

189

Charlayne Hunter and Hamilton Holmes, both graduates of Henry McNeal Turner High School, were the first African-Americans to integrate the University of Georgia in 1961.

T. Maurice Pennington served as a photographer and artist for the Atlanta Inquirer *newspaper during the 1960s.*

A. R. Simons captured many of the events of the civil rights movement in Atlanta. His works appeared in the black newspaper and other publications. He also did commercial work.

SIDEWALK CENSUS

Since Atlanta Negro High schools are severly over-crowded, do you feel that the pupil placement plan should be replaced by a plan that woul assure a more equal distribution of students?

BY JULIUS ALEXANDER

Julius Alexander worked as photographer for the Atlanta Inquirer *and created the "Sidewalk Census" column.*

Lawrence Jefferson and May McMullen leave Grady High School quietly after becoming the first two African-American students to integrate it in September 1961.

Thomas Welch and Madelyn Nix approach Brown High School as they become the first African-Americans to attend the school, c. 1961.

Willie Jean Black, Arthur Simmons, and Donita Gaines leave Northside High School after the first day of class, 1961.

Sheriff's deputies evict protestors from an unidentified school, c. 1969.

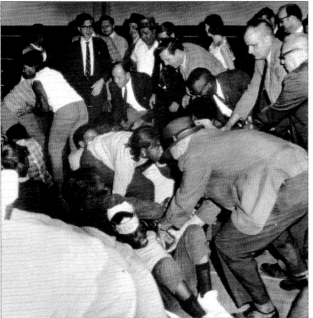

A peaceful march down Auburn Avenue from Peachtree. Fourth from right is Carolyn Long, an activist in the Atlanta civil rights movement and member of the Student Nonviolent Coordinating Committee. Long, who has served on the Atlanta City Council since 1980, was the first African-American woman to do so.

Atlanta University Center students are escorted to police cars following an incident inside the state capitol, 1962.

White Atlantans observe the attempts of African-American students to be served in this unidentified lunchroom, 1960.

Dr. Martin Luther King, Jr., and three other protestors are arrested at Rich's department store following sit-in demonstrations at several stores protesting lunch-counter segregation, c. 1960.

Rich's department store was the target of much demonstration and picketing, due to its practice of segregation. Here Thomas Reese marches in front of the store during the Christmas holiday season as white shoppers look on.

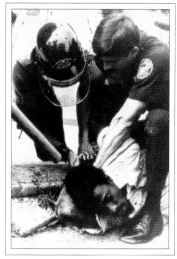

Scenes from the riot in the Summerhill community.

Mayor Ivan Allen intervenes in the Summerhill riot, during which one African-American man was killed and three others were wounded. A protest march was led by Stokely Carmichael and eventually resulted in another riot, 1966.

African-American dentists picket the American Dental Association's convention at the Municipal Auditorium in which they were not allowed to participate.

Chanting "black power" and waving placards, over three hundred African-Americans crowd a church in northeast Atlanta following two nights of rioting in the community, 1966.

In a rare instance where he was photographed smiling, Malcolm X mingles with a group of Clark College students after speaking to them in 1963.

Integration of Piedmont Park swimming pool, 1963.

Former First Lady Eleanor Roosevelt poses with (l–r) Vice-Mayor Sam Massell, Margaret Davis Bowen, Atlanta University president Dr. Rufus E. Clement, Lazette Hale, and Suzette Fountain Crank during a visit to Atlanta in 1962.

The Links inducted Coretta Scott King and Marge Yancey (who would later be elected to the Board of Education) to its social and civic organization during the 1960s.

Mayor Ivan Allen swears in attorney R. Prudence Herndon as the first African-American female judge.

This view looking north from Piedmont across Auburn Avenue captures the Rucker Building, the oldest office building in Atlanta for African-Americans, constructed in 1904 by Henry Rucker. One business in the building was House of Murphy Printers, founded by Harry S. Murphy in the late 1920s. Murphy purchased equipment from the ill-fated Standard Printing Company, a business concern once owned by Heman Perry. In the 1980s House of Murphy Printers moved to Edgewood Avenue and is now owned by Mrs. Katherine Jefferson, who began her career there in the 1940s.

Andrew "Count" Jackson began taking pictures at the Royal Peacock. He later opened a studio across the street from the club and photographed events in the African-American community during the 1960s and 1970s.

Citizens Trust Bank president congratulates longtime Auburn Avenue businessman William L. Calloway, as Atlanta Life executive Walter H. Smith looks on.

Irwin Favors, owner of the Auburn Avenue Casino Night Club, sponsored an annual Christmas Toy Drive for needy African-American children in the 1960s.

When B. B. Beamon decided to curtail his activity in the promoting and entertainment business, he opened a very popular restaurant on Auburn Avenue.

The Bankhead Drive-In Theatre was one of the first drive-ins in Atlanta to admit African-Americans.

In 1963 on a visit to Atlanta, Cassius Clay attended the annual Turkey Day Classic football game between Morris Brown and Clark. Clay (a.k.a. Muhammad Ali) would become a frequent visitor to Atlanta and in 1971 staged his comeback fight with Jerry Quarry at the Municipal Auditorium.

As African-Americans began to move to the west side in areas such as Adamsville and Collier Heights, religious institutions began to flourish. The West Side Community C.M.E. Church, on the corner of Gordon Road and Larwood, was completed in 1963.

These sisters play in front of their home in the new Carroll Heights subdivision located off of Bolton Road, 1963.

Attorneys Horace Ward and Leroy Johnson take the oath as they are sworn in to the Georgia Senate, c. 1965.

Johnson's Supermarket on Gordon Road near Delmar Lane, 1960.

Celebrities and dignitaries flocked to
Atlanta in support of the civil rights
movement led by Dr. Martin Luther
King, Jr. Here (top) King is embraced
by Sidney Poitier, the first African-
American to win an Academy Award.
Governor Nelson Rockefeller of New
York (bottom) is welcomed to Atlanta
by Dr. Benjamin E. Mays, Yolanda
King, Martin and Coretta King, Mrs.
Jackie Robinson, and Mayor Ivan
Allen. Jackie Robinson is hidden
behind Governor Rockefeller, c. 1965.
King and his father (center) chat dur-
ing the Biracial Dinner to celebrate
King's Nobel Peace Prize in 1964.

The King children at home (l–r): Martin Luther King III, Dexter, and Yolanda, c. 1963.

Graham Jackson, a legend in Atlanta's entertainment history, extends his hand to President Lyndon B. Johnson during a visit to Atlanta in 1964. Graham was a favorite guest of President Franklin D. Roosevelt at the "Little White House" in Warm Springs, Georgia.

Once a batboy for the Atlanta Black Crackers and a sensational ball player for several Negro league teams, Othello "Chico" Renfroe became Atlanta's premier sports broadcaster and journalist for African-American sports across the South. He succeeded Marion Jackson, who wrote the "Sports of the World" column for the Atlanta Daily World newspaper.

Former Atlanta Braves outfielder Rico Carty served as a spokesman for the Christmas Seals campaign, c. 1968.

Donn Clendenon, a graduate of Washington High School and Morehouse College, signed with the Pittsburgh Pirates in 1962. In 1963, he led the National League in double plays and in 1968 set a National League record for consecutive years in double plays for first baseman. After retiring in 1969, he joined the Atlanta firm Scripto, Inc., as vice-president of public relations and opened a night club on Hunter Street.

The construction of the Atlanta Stadium displaced thousands of residents in the Summerhill Community.

ABC Sports anchor Howard Cosell interviews Braves player Hank Aaron and San Francisco Giants player Willie Mays at the Atlanta Stadium.

Lou Hudson (right) was one of the early members of the Atlanta Hawks.

Former middleweight boxer Sugar Ray Robinson makes a visit to Atlanta and checks out Atlanta *magazine.*

Later crowned the "Godfather of Soul," James Brown and his band the Famous Flames began performing in Atlanta in the 1950s. As his popularity grew, so did the need for a larger venue to hold his concerts. After the Atlanta Stadium was completed in 1965, Brown and his revue became one of the first African-American entertainers to perform in the stadium.

The Calloway Building, named for William L. Calloway, long-time real estate magnate and the first African-American to open a loan company in Atlanta, was built next to the Citizens Trust Bank on Hunter Street.

Integration of the Grady Hospital medical facilities came in 1965. Theretofore, African-Americans were treated in a separate wing of the hospital or at the Hugh Spaulding Pavilion. Medical services were also provided at the privately owned McLendon Hospital, which was opened in 1949 by Dr. F. Earl McLendon. It was located on Sharon Street, off of Hunter Street, in the heart of the African-American middle-class community.

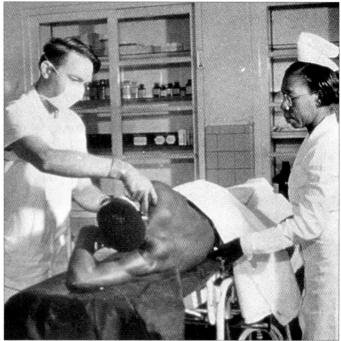

Theodore M. Alexander, seated on a chaise longue, and his family enjoy a poolside gathering at their home on Hunter Street in the 1960s. Alexander was the first African-American to run for political office in Atlanta since 1870.

Hunter Street, the black business district of the west side of Atlanta, was also a street for parades. The Atlanta University Center schools homecoming parades would take the traditional parade route from their respective campuses to Ashby Street then to Hunter Street. In the background are several businesses, including Williams Tavern and Beale's Laundry and Dry Cleaning.

African-American state legislators: (l–r) Julius Daugherty, William Alexander, Julian Bond, Ben Brown, Grace Towns Hamilton

The Atlanta Transit Authority has served the African-American community amicably in its bus service. Here, crossing Northside Drive, the Magnolia Street bus passes Mount Hermon Baptist Church, 1962.

Andrew Young listens as Dr. Martin Luther King, Jr., speaks to the media during a press conference in 1967.

Many African-American newspapers have a society columnist who chronicles the community's teas, weddings, births, and other goings on. Such columnists for the Atlanta Daily World *have included Lucius "Melancholy" Jones, Alice Maree, Alice Washington, Marjorie Fowlkes, and, pictured here, Oziel Fryer Woolcock, who wrote "Society Slants" for more than twenty years. At the* Atlanta Inquirer, *columnists have included Jondelle Johnson and M. Pauline Morgan White, who currently writes* • "Sparkling Specialties."

Surrounded by white photographers, Harmon Perry became the first African-American journalist for the Atlanta Journal *in 1968. His first assignment was to cover the assassination of Dr. Martin Luther King, Jr.*

Young attorney Maynard H. Jackson participates in a parade down Peachtree Street as he campaigns for the vice-mayor position in 1968.

Cupping his hand to his ear is Senator Eugene Talmadge, and seated next to him are businessman Clayton R. Yates; William A. Fowlkes, coordinator of Hungry Club activities and journalist; and Dr. Benjamin Elijah Mays, president of Morehouse College.

A scene from Ebenezer Baptist Church during Martin Luther King, Jr.'s funeral services on April 9, 1968.

Dr. King's interment was held at the Southview Cemetery on Jonesboro Road. The body was later entombed at a spot near Ebenezer Baptist Church, which would become the Martin Luther King, Jr., Center for Non-Violent Social Change.

This aerial view of the Atlanta University Center shows the massive number of mourners on the campus during Dr. King's memorial service, c. 1968.

Dr. Hugh M. Gloster (right), newly inaugurated president of Morehouse College, confers an honorary degree.

Maynard Holbrook Jackson is sworn in as vice-mayor of Atlanta by Mayor Sam Massell at city hall, 1968.

Teacher integration began to take place in 1968 throughout the Atlanta Public School System.

Lo Jelks became one of the first African-Americans in Atlanta to work for a local television station as a cameraman. He is now the editor and publisher of the AUC Digest.

Holding the key to the city, Mayor Sam Massell welcomes an unidentified delegation to Atlanta as they arrive at Hartsfield Airport. Pictured are numerous social and civic leaders and business owners, including Geneva Haugabrooks (seated in wheelchair); Mattiwilda Dobbs, famed opera singer; directly behind her Evelyn Frazier, owner of Frazier's Café Society on Hunter Street; and fifth from right, Margaret Davis Bowen, wife of Bishop J. W. E. Bowen and past national Basileus of Alpha Kappa Alpha sorority.

Chapter 10

"Deep in My Heart, I Do Believe, We Shall Overcome," 1970–1979

*N*egroes have been pursuing the dream of equality. That's what "black power" means. Putting some money in my pocket, some food on my table, and some dignity in my hand.

William Booth,
Commission on Human Rights

CHRONOLOGY

1970   January. Five African-Americans are elected or re-elected to the eighteen-member Board of Aldermen (city council), and three are elected to the Board of Education.

Emma Darnell is featured on the cover of *Jet*.

Attorney Romae Powell is appointed as the first African-American female judge of Juvenile Courts in Atlanta. She is a graduate of Spelman College and the Howard University School of Law.

1971   January. An African-American attorney, Howard Moore, represents Angela Davis, who has been charged with murder, kidnapping, and criminal conspiracy.

Whitney Young, the former dean of the School of Social Work at Atlanta University, dies in Nigeria. (Young had left the university in 1961 to become executive director of the National Urban League. Native Atlantan and attorney Vernon E. Jordan, Jr., succeeded Young as executive director.)

Muhammad Ali stages his comeback fight in Atlanta after the U.S. Supreme Court overturns his conviction for draft evasion.

1972   Twenty-six African-American parents participate in a suit filed by the American Civil Liberties Union demanding that a metro-wide school desegregation plan be developed.

Andrew Jackson Young, former aide to Martin Luther King, Jr., is elected to the U.S. Congress from the Fifth District of Georgia, which includes Atlanta. He is the first African-American since Reconstruction to hold that office. (He was reelected in 1974 and 1976.)

Johnnie Labot Yancey, the first African-American to serve on the Board of Trustees for the Atlanta Public Library, dies.

1973   WSB Radio airs "Black Almanac," featuring leaders and citizens talking about the problems and successes of African-American Atlantans.

Rich's department store denies charges of discrimination as a group of two hundred demonstrators protests in front of the downtown store.

Wheat Street Towers, a high rise for senior citizens, is opened.

Alonzo A. Crim is selected to serve as the first African-American superintendent of the Atlanta Public School System. Ninety percent of the school children are African-American.

1974   February. MARTA begins clearing land in the Washington Heights community for the construction of the Ashby Street Rapid Rail Station.

April 18. Henry "Hank" Aaron, outfielder for the Atlanta Braves, hits his 715th career home run, breaking the record previously held by Babe Ruth. The historic event takes place at the Atlanta Stadium.

Hank Aaron

May 27. Reacting to reports of police brutality, demonstrators marching through downtown Atlanta demand that Police Chief John Inman be fired. More than one thousand people are led by Hosea Williams, a former top aide to Martin Luther King, Jr. Mayor Jackson attempts to fire Inman but is prohibited by a judge in the DeKalb County Superior Court.

June 26. African-American marchers protest the killing of a seventeen-year-old youth by police and continue to demand the dismissal of Police Chief Inman. Of the 250 marchers, 14 are arrested and charged with parading without a permit.

Maynard H. Jackson is sworn in as the first African-American mayor of Atlanta.

Protest march against Police Chief John Inman.

A portrait of Dr. Martin Luther King, Jr., is unveiled in the Georgia state capitol, making King the first African-American leader to be represented in the state's official portrait gallery.

Alberta Williams King, mother of Dr. Martin Luther King, Jr., is shot and killed while playing "The Lord's Prayer" during a worship service at Ebenezer Baptist Church. (The gunman was Marcus Chenault of Dayton, Ohio.)

George Alexander Towns Elementary School becomes the first public building in the United States to have a solar cooling and heating system.

The Georgia Power Company pays retroactive wages and pension benefits to African-American employees who have been denied equal job rights five years after a law suit was filed by the U.S. Department of Justice. African-American employment is increased.

1975   January. Edward L. Baty, a 30-year-old attorney and graduate of Morris Brown College and Howard University, is appointed as the first full-time African-American municipal traffic judge. Mary Welcome, a 31-year-old attorney who graduated from Howard University, is named municipal court solicitor. Both appointments are made by Mayor Jackson.

January. Over three thousand young African-Americans crash into the glass doors at the Atlanta Civic Center as they attempt to apply for 225 public service jobs, causing injuries.

The movie *Let's Do It Again* is filmed on Auburn Avenue at Big Bethel A.M.E. Church. The film is directed by Sidney Poitier and features Bill Cosby. Other filming takes place at the Atlanta City Hall and at the corner of Adridge and Chappell Road in the Hunter Hill community.

The Atlanta Fire Department is targeted by the U.S. Justice Department for discriminating against African-American employees by refusing to hire them prior to 1964, using unfair promotion tests.

The Campbellton Road strip features the largest and liveliest selection of night spots for African-Americans in Atlanta. Clubs such as Mr. V's Figure 8, Cisco's, and Marko's Disco and Restaurant provide urbanites with social outlets. Nestled between three shopping centers—Greenbriar, Westgate, and Delowe Plaza—Campbellton Road has numerous fast-food restaurants, auto showrooms, bank branches, gas stations, package stores, and convenience shops.

Monica Kaufman becomes the first African-American woman to anchor a newscast in Atlanta.

Reverend Ike appears at the Omni.

April. The Black Christian Nationalist Church (BCN) holds its Third Biennial National Convention in Atlanta.

The Atlanta Braves appoint William "Bill" Lucas as director of player personnel, the highest position ever held by an African-American in professional baseball.

Monica Kaufman

1976   February. A portrait of Selena Sloan Butler is added to the gallery at the state capitol.

Jesse Hill, president of Atlanta Life Insurance Company, is the first African-American elected president of the Atlanta Chamber of Commerce.

Just Us Theater Company, an African-American theater company, is formed as part of the Theater of the Stars and developed from the Black Image Theater and the New Cosmos Theater. (Throughout its tenure, it presented to the stage plays such as *A Raisin in the Sun*, *Timbuktu*, *Purlie*, *Ain't Misbehavin'*, *Eubie*, *The Black Nativity*, and *Bubbling Brown Sugar*.)

1977   April. Horace Ward is appointed to the Fulton County Superior Court.

Jesse Hill is elected as the first African-American member of the Atlanta Chamber of Commerce.

Ezra Johnson, defensive end at Morris Brown College, becomes the first football player from an Atlanta University Center School to be selected in the first round of the National

Football League draft. Johnson is drafted by the Green Bay Packers.

April. James Alan McPherson, a 1965 graduate of Morris Brown College, is awarded a Pulitzer Prize in fiction for his volume of short stories, *Elbow Room*.

Ezra Johnson

1979   The Atlanta Missing and Murdered Children saga begins. (In the next two years, twenty-eight young African-Americans would be slain. Atlanta received national attention. On February 27, 1982, Wayne Williams was convicted of murder in the slaying of two of the twenty-eight.)

Maynard Jackson begins his second term of office.

Benjamin E. Mays, president of the Atlanta Board of Education, rejects the idea of "massive busing."

Jomandi Production Theater Company is founded by Tom Jones and Marsha Jackson. The company produces new works by African-American playwrights.

Ebony magazine cites Atlanta as one of the ten best cities for African-Americans.

The Hightower Medical and Dental Clinic opens.

Henry D. Dodson photographed the African-American community in Atlanta in the 1960s and 1970s. After he put his camera down, he went into politics and was elected to the Fulton County Board of Commissioners.

Q. V. Williamson (seated), dean of the African-Americans on the Atlanta City Council, is shown with the other African-American members (l–r): James Howard, Morris Finley, Marvin Arrington, Carl Ware, Ira Jackson, James Bond, and John Calhoun.

Atlanta Board of Education president Benjamin E. Mays (left) confers with Mayor Sam Massell (center) and construction magnate Herman Russell (right) following a session at the Hungry Club.

Mayor Sam Massell takes a tour of the Atlanta Voice *printing plant. Left to right are Alyce Ware, founder and editor J. Lowell Ware, Mayor Massell, and an unidentified man. The* Atlanta Voice *became the fourth African-American-owned newspaper in Atlanta.*

Thousands of Atlanta's African-Americans converged on Peachtree Street to welcome Richard Nixon to Atlanta.

Angela Davis, escorted by Rev. Ralph David Abernathy, prepares to enter Wheat Street Baptist Church for a conference.

In 1973, Eddie McAshan was the first African-American quarterback on the Georgia Tech football team. He is pictured with teammates and coach after accepting the invitation to participate in the Peach Bowl.

Jesse Jackson and Julian Bond strategize at Paschal's Restaurant, the "unofficial boardroom" of the civil rights movement.

Since the 1950s Bronner Brothers has sponsored an annual beauty and trade show, featuring a fashion show and revue. Participants in the early 1970s pose with the Bronner Brothers, family, and staff members.

Before Edwin Moses won the 400-meter intermediate hurdles at the Olympic Games, he refined his skills as an all-star track-and-field runner for Morehouse College. The track at the B. T. Harvey Stadium was named for Moses.

Rev. Martin Luther King, Sr., mourns the death of his wife, Alberta "Mama" King, during the funeral services at Ebenezer Baptist Church, 1974.

The city of Atlanta mourned once more for the King family as they lined Auburn Avenue to view the body of Alberta "Mama" King, who was killed during a Sunday morning worship service, c. 1974.

Actors Bill Cosby and Sidney Poitier, in town to film Let's Do It Again, *listen to Mayor Maynard H. Jackson on the steps of Atlanta's city hall, c. 1974.*

Atlanta's African-American Muslim community begins to assemble outside of the Municipal Auditorium for the closed-circuit viewing of a message given by the Honorable Elijah Muhammad, 1975.

The Morehouse College Glee Club, organized in 1911, performs with the Atlanta Symphony Orchestra in the school's gymnasium.

The City of Atlanta Firefighters meet with Mayor Jackson and other officials regarding an agreement in a five-year-old discrimination suit filed by African-American firefighters, c. 1979.

Hunter Street, Mozley Drive, and Gordon Road were together renamed Martin Luther King, Jr., Drive. Mayor Jackson, Coretta Scott King, Ralph David Abernathy, and Q. V. Williamson participate in the unveiling of the street signs, c. 1976.

Having performed for more than twenty-five years, native Atlantans Gladys Knight and the Pips (William Patton, Edward Guest, and Merald Knight) were internationally known.

An African-American police officer and her partner walk their beat. This was a clear sign of internal progress on the police force.

The bronze statue of home-run king Hank Aaron, by African-American sculptor Ed Dwight, is unveiled at the Atlanta Stadium. Aaron is surrounded by hundreds of well-wishers and the media.

Chapter 11

"Still a City Too Busy to Hate"
1980–1989

I feel like reaching for the sky. I'm so inspired, I want to reach a little higher.

Peabo Bryson, singer and Atlanta resident

CHRONOLOGY

1980   January. Attorney Thelma Wyatt Cummings is appointed judge in the city's municipal court.

April. Carolyn Long Banks is elected as the first African-American woman to the Atlanta City Council. (During her college days at Clark College, Banks was very active in the Student Nonviolent Coordinating Commission [SNCC].)

The Atlanta Branch of the NAACP supports gun control but opposes the changing of the Atlanta City Charter.

Marvin Arrington and Michael Lomax face a runoff for president of the city council. Arrington wins.

The International Business Institute is established at Atlanta University.

An act of Congress declares portions of the Auburn community—including the King Birth Home—the Martin Luther King, Jr., National Historic District.

Herndon Plaza, the headquarters of the Atlanta Life Insurance Company, is completed.

1981   Mayor Maynard Jackson and the Atlanta City Council disagree over the need for more police.

One of the mayoral candidates is former police chief A. Reginald Eaves.

MARTA completes housing for hundreds of African-Americans who were displaced by the construction of the tracks.

Techwood residents begin patrolling their own projects in lieu of the unrest surrounding the missing and murdered children saga.

Morris Brown and Spelman colleges celebrate the centennial anniversary of their respected schools.

Michael Lomax is elected as the first African-American Fulton County commissioner.

Mrs. Willie Kate Jones, who led the struggle to obtain employment benefits for cafeteria workers of the Atlanta Board of Education, dies.

1982   January. Andrew Young is elected mayor of Atlanta.

March. Wayne Williams is convicted on two counts of murder in the most sensationalized and publicized trial in the history of African-Americans in Atlanta. The judge is Clarence Cooper, a graduate of Clark College.

Beverly Harvard, a graduate of Morris Brown College, is named the first African-American woman to serve as deputy police chief.

The Atlanta Board of Education votes to close down ten schools, all of which will displace African-American students and relocate them to other schools.

Atlanta police chief Lee Brown leaves Atlanta for Houston.

William Harner is named chief of the Atlanta Fire Department, the first African-American to hold that office.

Andrew Jackson Young is elected as the second African-American mayor in Atlanta.

1983   The National Baptist Convention erects a statue of Dr. Martin Luther King, Jr., on the Morehouse College campus.

1984   March 28. Dr. Benjamin E. Mays dies.

Three hundred Atlanta city employees demonstrate for a pay raise.

Atlanta native Michael Hollis, a graduate of Booker T. Washington High School, launches Air Atlanta, becoming the first African-American founder and chair of a U.S. airline.

Dr. Martin Luther King, Sr., dies.

1985   A portion of Yonge Street is renamed for Rev. William Holmes Borders.

The memorial statue of Charles Lincoln Harper, principal of Booker T. Washington High School, is unveiled.

Collection of Life and Heritage, Inc., opens Phase I of a two-phase project to establish a national African-American art and history museum.

Atlanta and the nation celebrate the first national holiday in honor of slain civil rights leader Dr. Martin Luther King, Jr.

1986   Jesse L. Jackson addresses 11,000 people at the Democratic National Convention in Atlanta. (Jackson was one of two African-American nominees for president. The other was Lenora Fulani.)

1987   Johnetta Betsch Cole, Ph.D., is selected as the first African-American female president of Spelman College.

The Lightning Landowner Association and business owners of southeast Atlanta meet with the Atlanta City Council Human Services Division to discuss concerns over the proposed Georgia Dome, including relocation compensation for homeowners.

The Atlanta Bureau of Cultural Affairs, Atlanta Third World Film Festival, and the National Black Arts Festival present the Black Cinematheque, a celebration of black independent films.

The Atlanta Fulton Public Library Board of Trustees approves a new site on Auburn Avenue for a proposed research library.

Pioneer librarian Annie L. McPheeters publishes *Library Services in Black and White*, a history of the development of library services for African-Americans in Atlanta.

1988   The city of Atlanta and Fulton County inaugurate and host the first National Black Arts Festival, featuring two weeks of cultural performances, artist markets, and exhibits.

1989   January. J. Jerome Harris is selected as the superintendent of the Atlanta public schools, the second African-American to serve in this position.

January. Ku Klux Klan are escorted by police and national guardsmen through a crowd of more than 3,000 African-American demonstrators at the Georgia state capitol.

March. The Georgia Supreme Court overturns a ruling that established a model program for steering contracts to minority businesses.

May. All sixty-four savings and loans banks in the Atlanta metropolitan area are under investigation for charges of discrimination against African-Americans and Hispanics.

July. Clark College and Atlanta University merge to become Clark Atlanta University. Thomas W. Cole, Jr., Ph.D., is president.

Atlanta mayor Andrew Young announces his candidacy for governor of Georgia.

Atlanta native Louis Sullivan, president of the Morehouse School of Medicine, accepts the nomination from President George Bush to serve as secretary of health and human services.

Oprah Winfrey donates $1 million to Morehouse College to establish the Oprah Winfrey Scholarship Fund.

Student unrest at Morris Brown College results in twenty-five students barricading themselves in front of the administration building and presenting a list of demands to the school's administration.

Louis W. Sullivan is confirmed as secretary of health and human services by the U.S. Senate. (Sullivan, a 1954 graduate of Morehouse College, was named dean of the School of Medicine in 1974 and president in 1976.)

Before he became chief of police, Eldrin Bell worked his way through the ranks and was actively involved in the search for Atlanta's missing and murdered children. Here he holds up a handbill to the media describing the latest missing child, c. 1981.

The body of one of the missing and murdered children being carried out of the church.

With over forty years of service to the community as owners of a restaurant and hotel, the Paschal brothers—James, Gill, and Robert—embrace, c. 1984.

Dr. Benjamin E. Mays (center) signs a document endorsing the Collection of Life and Heritage Museum. Witnessing this historic event are Henry "Hank" Aaron (standing); Dan Moore, founder and president of the museum; and Alonzo A. Crim, superintendent of the Atlanta Public School System.

Atlanta public school graduations have come a long way since the early days in the old City Auditorium, where young women wore white dresses and young men wore dark suits. Graduations include eloquent oratory from top students, singing, and props to illustrate the songs' message. Here, the Therell High School class of '85, whose class song was "We Are the World," receives degrees beneath a large suspended globe at the Atlanta Civic Center, c. 1985.

Andrew Jackson Young, Atlanta's second African-American mayor, speaks to demonstrators who have gathered in the rain to protest apartheid, c. 1986.

Former city councilman John H. Calhoun (right) points out some facts to another former councilman, Hosea Williams (left), as Butler Street YMCA director Dewitt Martin (center) looks on, 1983.

Surrounded by local media are state senator Julian Bond; Joseph Lowery, president of the SCLC; and Representative Tyrone Brooks, speaking on the steps of the state capitol. They were blasting President Ronald Reagan's South African policy, c. 1981.

Flanking the tomb of Dr. King are Dr. Benjamin E. Mays; Rev. King, Sr.; Jesse Hill, chairman of the Board of the King Center for Non-Violent Social Change and president of Atlanta Life; and Coretta Scott King, 1983.

Before becoming heavyweight boxing champion of the world, Evander Holyfield devoted some of his time as an instructor at the Warren Memorial Boys Club, where he received his early training, c. 1985.

William Herty Killian, known throughout Atlanta as "Coach," photographed the Atlanta University Center sports teams and edited a column in the Atlanta Voice newspaper until his death in 1990.

Ben Hill United Methodist Church in southwest Atlanta once had a predominately white membership and cemetery. The church received its first African-American minister in 1974 and had a congregation of 500. In five years the membership grew to 2,000, and by the end of the 1980s it totaled more than 5,000, making it one of the fastest-growing churches in Georgia.

Chapter 12

Going for the Gold, 1990–Present

*It is not your environment, it is you—the quality of your minds,
the integrity of your souls, and the determination of your wills—
that will decide your future and shape your lives.*

Benjamin E. Mays

CHRONOLOGY

1990   Nelson Mandela, after being released from prison, begins a world tour, which includes a stop in Atlanta. Mandela speaks to a standing-room-only crowd at the Georgia Tech Bobby Dodd Stadium.

Actors Cicely Tyson and Harry Belafonte are named co-chairs for the 1990 National Black Arts Festival.

Andrew Young loses his bid for governor against Zell Miller.

Maynard H. Jackson is elected to the Office of Mayor after having served a previous eight-year term from 1974 to 1982.

The city of Atlanta is awarded the opportunity to host the 1996 Centennial Games of the Olympiad.

Kenny Leon, a graduate of Clark College, is named the first African-American artistic director of the Alliance Theater.

1991   A not-guilty verdict is given in the Rodney King trial in Los Angeles. Riot and unrest erupts. In Atlanta, the Atlanta University Center students take to the streets and march in protest of the verdict. Atlanta policemen retaliate in a clash of tear gas and violence on Fair Street. Sixty-eight arrests are made, both of students and individuals from the surrounding commnities of Buttermilk Bottom and the John Hope/University Homes.

Valerie Richardson Jackson watches as Judge Leah Sears-Collins administers the oath of office to her husband, Mayor-elect Maynard Jackson. Judge Collins is the first African-American female justice of the Supreme Court of Georgia.

Since 1962, African-Americans have been a part of the Atlanta fire department. The first fire station to house African-American firemen was located on Simpson Road on the site of the home of middleweight boxing champion "Tiger" Flowers, whose home was demolished to build the firestation.

The Atlanta Police Department opened a precinct in the remodeled building that once served as a gas station and dry cleaners on the corner of Auburn Avenue and Bell Street.

The block of historic Auburn Avenue between Fort and Hilliard streets.

Filmmaker and former
Atlantan Spike Lee

The King Tomb,
Ebenezer Baptist
Church, and M. L.
King National Historic
Site are among the most
visited sites in Georgia.

The world-renowned Morris Brown College Marching Wolverines Band,
under the direction of Cleopas Johnson, has performed throughout the country, bringing acclaim to the Atlanta school.

Nelson Mandela visited Atlanta during his international world tour following his release from a South African prison, 1990.

A celebration of dance during the National Black Arts Festival.

Michael Lomax, who in 1981 became the first African-American chairman of the Fulton County Commission, gave birth to the National Black Arts Festival, a week-long cultural escape exploring the richness of African-American art, music, dance, and theater. He is flanked by Mayor Maynard Jackson.

Atlanta mayor Andrew Young announces his candidacy for governor of Georgia in 1989 as his wife, Jean, looks on.

State Senator Tyrone Brooks and Congressman John Lewis march in the first Brother's Day Rally in 1990.

The John Wesley Dobbs Building, a former book repository, is the home of the Southern Education Foundation and the African-American Panoramic Experience Museum (APEX).

Since the late 1960s, the Atlanta Hawks have displayed outstanding African-American talent on the hardwood. Here Kevin Willis is embraced by Dominique Wilkins following action at the Omni Coliseum, c. 1991.

Falcons (l–r) Andre Rison, Michael Haynes, and George Thomas celebrate Haynes's game-winning catch in the fourth quarter on a "Hail Mary" play that lifted the Falcons over the 49ers, 17–14.

(L–r) Chris Chambliss observes Deion Sanders, David Justice, and Ron Gant during an Atlanta Braves baseball team practice. The players are members of the two-time National League Championship team.

Evander Holyfield holds his championship belt high as he rides down Peachtree Street in an afternoon parade in his honor. Holyfield is the second African-American from Atlanta to win a national boxing championship, the first being Theodore "Tiger" Flowers, who became the first African-American to win the middleweight boxing championship in 1926.

When Underground Atlanta reopened in 1989, it became a mecca for African-American businesses and entrepreneurs. African art shops, clothing stores, restaurants, and gift and novelty shops are a sampling of the businesses, c. 1990.

Enjoying an outing at Piedmont Park.

The Georgia Dome was constructed in the former African-American community called Lightning. It sits across the street from the Vine City community.

Auburn Avenue's "Golden Lady" Kathleen Redding Adams, who was born on this street in 1890.

Kenny Leon (right) and Tom Jones (left) perform in the Jomandi Production That Serious He Man Ball. *Leon became the first African-American artistic director for the Alliance Theater.*

The U.S. flag and the Confederate flag blowing in the wind. . . . African-Americans are still "going against the wind."

BIBLIOGRAPHY

Books and Articles

Bacote, Clarence A. *The Story of Atlanta University*. Atlanta: Atlanta University, 1969.

Bond, Julian. *A Time to Speak, A Time to Act*. New York: Simon and Schuster, 1972.

Brawley, Benjamin. *A History of Morehouse College*. Atlanta: Morehouse College, 1917.

Brawley, James P. *The Clark College Legacy*. Atlanta: Clark College, 1977.

Buckley, Gail Lumet. *The Hornes: An American Family*. New York: Alfred A. Knopf, 1986.

Carter, Edward Randolph. *The Black Side*. Atlanta, 1894.

DuBois, William E. B. *The College-Bred Negro*. Atlanta: Atlanta University Press, 1907.

————. *The Negro American Family*. Atlanta: Atlanta University Press, 1908.

Durett, Dan, and Dana White, *Another Atlanta: The Black Heritage*. Atlanta: Western Publishing Co., 1975.

English, James. *Handyman of the Lord: The Life and Ministry of the Reverend William Holmes Borders*. New York: Meredith Press, 1967.

Garrett, Franklin M. *Atlanta and Environs: A Chronicle of Its People and Events*. 2 vols. New York: Lewis Historical Publishing Company, 1954.

————. *Yesterday's Atlanta*. New York: Lewis Historical Publishing Company, 1954.

Gordon, Asa. *The Georgia Negro: A History*. Ann Arbor, Mich.: Edwards Brother, Inc., 1937.

Harlshorn, W. N. *An Era of Progress and Promise, 1863–1919*. The Clifton Conference. Priscilla Publishing Company, 1910.

Henderson, Alexa B. "Alonzo F. Herndon and Black Insurance in Atlanta, 1904–15." *Atlanta Historical Bulletin* 21 (Spring 1977): 34–47.

————. *Atlanta Life Insurance Company, Guardian of Black Economic Dignity*. Tuscaloosa: University of Alabama Press, 1990.

Hornsby, Alton, Jr. *Chronology of African-American History: Significant Events and People from 1619 to the Present*. Detroit: Gale Research, Inc., 1991.

Jones, Edward. *A Candle in the Dark: A History of Morehouse College*. Valley Forge: Judson Press, 1967.

Kuhn, Clifford M., and Harlon E. Joyce. *Living Atlanta: An Oral History of the City, 1914–1948*. Atlanta: Atlanta Historical Society, 1988.

McPheeters, Annie B. *Negro Progress in Atlanta, Georgia, 1950–60, 1960–70*. Atlanta: Atlanta Public Library, 1964.

Mullis, Sharon Mitchell. *The Public Career of Grace Towns Hamilton: A Citizen Too Busy To Hate*. Ann Arbor, Mich.: Xerox University Microfilms, 1976.

Read, Florence M. *The Story of Spelman College*. Princeton: Princeton University Press, 1961.

Richardson, Clement, et al. *The National Cyclopedia of the Colored Race*. Tuskegee, Ala., 1918.

Rouse, Jacqueline Anne. *Lugenia Burns Hope: Black Southern Reformer*. Athens: University of Georgia Press, 1989.

Russell, James Michael. *Atlanta 1847–1890, City Building in the Old South and the New*. Baton Rouge: Louisiana State University Press, 1988.

Sewell, George A., and Cornelius V. Troup. *Morris Brown College: The First Hundred Years, 1881–1981*. Charlotte, N.C.: The Delmar Co., 1981.

Shavin, Norman. *Atlanta: Triumph of a People*. Atlanta: Capricorn Corporation, 1982.

————. *Days in the Life of Atlanta*. Atlanta: Capricorn Corporation, 1987.

Sheftall, Beverly, and Jo Moore Stewart. *Spelman: A Centennial Celebration, 1881–1981*. Charlotte, N.C.: The Delmar Co., 1981.

Stone, Clarence N. *Regime Politics: Governing Atlanta, 1946–1988*. Lawrence, Kans.: University Press of Kansas, 1989.

Vowels, Robert C. "Atlanta Negro Business and the New Black Bourgeoise." *Atlanta Historical Bulletin* 21 (Spring 1977): 48–63.

Weiss, Nancy J. *Whitney M. Young, Jr., and the Struggle for Civil Rights*. Princeton, N.J.: Princeton University Press, 1989.

Documents

Atlanta Public Library. Special Collections. Vertical File Collection. Atlanta, Georgia.

Behind These Doors. vol. 1. November 1970. Supplement to the *Aurora*. Sigma Gamma Rho Sorority.

Booker T. Washington High School Fiftieth Anniversary Souvenir Booklet, 1924–74.

Calloway, William L. *"The Sweet Auburn Avenue" Business History, 1890-1988*.

"A Century of Progress and Christian Service." Big Bethel A.M.E. Church, 1968.

"Community Building: The History of Atlanta University Neighborhoods."

Ebenezer: A Centennial Time Capsule, 1886–1986.

Friendship Baptist Church 125th Anniversary Celebration Souvenir Album.

Henderson, Alexa B. "A Quest for Economic Dignity: The Story of Atlanta Life, 1905–1980."

National Urban League Fortieth Anniversary Yearbook, 1951.

The Negro Business Directory and Commercial Guide of Atlanta, 1911.

Odd Fellows Auditorium Restoration Project Program, May 25, 1984.

Profiles of Summerhill, October 8, 1967.
Robert W. Woodruff Library, Special Collections. Vertical File Collection.
Souvenir Booklet, Butler Street Christian Methodist Episcopal Church, 1882–1977.
Souvenir Program of the National Association of Colored Graduate Nurses, June 15–21, 1947, Atlanta,Georgia.
Souvenir Program of the Sixth Annual Woman's Missionary Convention of Georgia of the Christian
      Methodist Episcopal Church, July 27–31, 1910.
"Sweet Auburn: The Thriving Hub of Black Atlanta." Martin Luther King, Jr., National Historic Site and
      Preservation District. Prepared by Dr. Alexa B. Henderson and Dr. Eugene Walker.
Wood, Lee Fuse. The Bedford Pine Neighborhood, 1987–1987. College Park: Ditto Press, 1988.

Yearbooks
City Directories. 1859–1960.
The Morehouse Tiger. 1925–26.

Periodicals
Atlanta Daily World, 1930–90
Atlanta Independent, 1903–29
Atlanta Inquirer
Atlanta Journal and Constitution
Ebony Magazine

Unpublished Documents
"Forging and Reforging A Successful Enterprise: The Rise, Fall, and Resurgence of Black Business on
      Auburn Avenue in Atlanta, Georgia, 1870–1988," by Olivia Butler.

PHOTOGRAPHY CREDITS

Many thanks to the organizations and individuals who allowed us to use photographs from their collections.

Organizations
The APEX Museum; Atlanta-Fulton Public Library; *Atlanta Journal and Constitution* Archives; Atlanta Historical Society; Herndon Foundation (Dr. Carole Merritt); House of Murphy Printers; Robert W. Woodruff Library Special Collections; Scurlock Studio, Washington, D.C.

Individuals
Kathleen Redding Adams; Emma Amos; Isaiah S. Blocker; Father Henry J. C. Bowden, Sr.; William L. Calloway; Harriet Nash Chisholm; Ann Cooper; Angela Dawson; Pearlie Dove; Clarence and Etta Ezzard; David Fulmer; Ellen Jean Hailey; Mamie Hailey; Annie Doris Hall; Mr. and Mrs. Frederick D. Hall, Jr.; Frederick C. Harris; Narvie Jordan Harris; Dorothy Howard Harrison; Mable Bingham Hawk; Alexa B. Henderson; Jacob R. Henderson; Mabel Henderson; Mamie Kelly Holmes; J. Arthur Kelly; Mable Jackson; Katherine Jefferson; Myron Johnson; Sylvia Harris Johnston; Georgia Jones; Ruby Jones; Darlene Killian; Rose Favors Lawson; Andrew J. Lewis (deceased); Clara Stanley Lowe; David McCord; Marybelle Mariano; Chris Mitchell; Daisy Parham; Dovie Patrick; Eleanor Hamilton Payne; George and Virginia Prather; Emmit Lacoste Proctor; Katie Reese; Julian H. Robinson (deceased); Harold Ross; Mattie Ross; Sonya Ross; Nonye Strong Shephard; Irene McTear Thomas; Albert N. Wardlaw; Alice Washington; Gladys Willingham

The "Hidden Treasures" Photographers:

Living	Deceased
Alexander Adams	Thomas Askew
Julius Alexander	Lucius Henderson
Griffith Davis	Herbert Hawkins
Carl Dickerson	Paul Poole
Henry D. Dodson	Andrew T. Kelly
Andrew "Count" Jackson	W. A. Scott III
Robert "Bob" Johnson	William H. Killian
T. M. Pennington	Charles W. Lowe
Harmon Perry	Thomas Reese
A. Raymond Simons	
Arthur "Bud" Smith	
Robert Spaulding	

ATLANTA JOURNAL AND CONSTITUTION PHOTOGRAPHERS
W. A. Bridges, Jr.; Johnny Crawford; Steve Deal; Billy Downs; Louie Favorite; Renee Hannans; Charles Jackson; Bill Mahan; Charles Pugh; Michael A. Schwarz; Andy Sharp; Bud Skinner; Hugh Stovall; Ray West; Bill Wilson